The First Oasth
in the V

GW00683359

The History of the Rainh

Rainham Theatrical Society
Oasthouse Theatre,
Stratford Lane,
Rainham,
Kent.

01634 372121

www.oasthousetheatre.co.uk

ISBN 0948193891
Published for the Rainham Theatrical Society by Meresborough
Books, 17 Station Road, Rainham, Kent ME8 7RS
Printed by Lanes Printers, Broadstairs.

Foreword

By Roy Hudd

Patron of the Rainham Theatrical Society

"They've been at it now for forty years and it don't seem a day too much". Almost the words of one of my favourite music hall songs, "My Old Dutch." But these words apply to one of my favourite amateur companies, the resident RATS at the Oasthouse Theatre, the Rainham Theatrical Society. Since an old pal of mine, Bob Nicholls, introduced me to the unique theatre and its company, the RATS have kept in touch and I've been amazed at the breadth of productions they tackle. They are a credit to amateur theatre. Their dedication, enthusiasm and lively social activities are what theatre, be it amateur or professional, is all about. Long may they continue.

The team who finally found time to write the history of the Oasthouse Theatre (from left) standing: Steve Berry, Dean Caston and David O'Brien and sitting: Beryl Lacey, Helen Caston and Sarah O'Brien. Between them this group have over 100 years of Oasthouse experience and have been involved in over 200 productions.

Introduction

"A great adventure in local amateur dramatics is slowly taking shape within a group of ramshackle buildings just off Rainham High Street." This was the message under the headline "Rainham amateurs' great adventure" which appeared in the local newspaper in Rainham in 1962.

The 'Great Adventure' was to turn a derelict Oasthouse into a theatre. By 9th November 1963, the first Oasthouse Theatre in the World was ready to open its doors to the public. Forty years later, the Rainham Theatrical Society (RaTS) is still entertaining packed houses at the Oasthouse Theatre – and this is our story.

The programme for our production of *Merry Switzerland* in 1966, said "We would like to tell you all about the history of the Oasthouse. Perhaps one day we will be able to. So far though, no one in the RATS has been able to spare the time to research into all this." This was a theme often repeated in programmes for the rest of the century. As we approached our 40th anniversary at the Oasthouse, a group of members finally took the bull by the horns and resolved to write the history of our charming and historic theatre.

Steve Berry, Beryl Lacey and husband and wife teams Dean & Helen Caston and David & Sarah O'Brien met on a regular basis for 10 months, pulling together all available material and drawing on the memories of some of the people who have contributed to the success of the Great Adventure.

We are particularly indebted to Brenda Pearson, the only person to have been an active (and valued) member for every one of our 40 years at the Oasthouse. Her diligence in collating material since she joined the RATS in 1961 has provided much of the factual information for this book.

Many other members past and present, too numerous to mention individually here, have provided printed material, memories, opinions and anecdotes. Our heartfelt thanks go to all who have helped with our research. The story is theirs – any errors are ours.

For those reading this book from further afield, Rainham is part of the Medway Towns in Kent and an Oasthouse is a building peculiar to this part of the world, designed for drying mature hops used in the beermaking process. The name derives from the latin word 'aestus' meaning heat and the buildings were introduced to Kent in the 16th century by Flemish weavers who brought new varieties of hops into the county when they arrived to work in its prosperous wool industry.

Despite our pride in our history, RaTS is very much a thriving and forward-looking society. In 1999, as a first step in to the 21st century, our chairman, Dean Caston, put forward a resolution to remove the word 'Amateur' from the society's name (formerly Rainham Amateur Theatrical Society), in order to reflect the high standards towards which we strive. The society decided that they wished to keep the pet name of "RATS" (no pun intended!) so it was agreed to use the second letter of Rainham instead and the new title became The Rainham Theatrical Society, or RaTS for short.

We also boast an excellent website and invite you to see colour photos of our theatre and news of our latest productions at www.oasthousetheatre.co.uk

But let's begin our story in the days when King George VI was on the throne and a website was a place where spiders gathered in the back garden .....

A Theatre of our own

Whilst November 2003 sees the 40th anniversary of the Rainham Theatrical Society at the Oasthouse Theatre, the group was originally founded back in 1948 and its origins can be traced back even further.

The group started out as 'The Toc-H Players' and was formed by members of the Rainham branch of Toc-H. (The Toc-H Association was formed by Royal Charter in 1922 to help support soldiers and victims who fought in the Ypres conflict during the First World War). Early records indicate that the first production, in 1946, was entitled *Husbands are a Problem*. It's good to see that some things haven't changed in over half a century!

As the popularity of the group grew, new members joined who were not involved with Toc-H and it was decided to find a new name for the blossoming company. After much discussion, the Rainham Amateur Theatrical Society was founded and the rest, as they say, is history!

The first production under the banner of the Rainham Amateur Theatrical Society (or RATS) was *Great Day* by Leslie Storm, which was performed on 1st & 3rd December 1948 in the Co-operative Hall in Rainham. This building was situated opposite St Margaret's Church and has since been demolished.

In the early days the group rehearsed in the Toc-H rooms in Rainham and a barn in Upchurch belonging to Brian Wakeley. As members became engrossed in rehearsals, they often missed the last bus (there was only one bus an hour) and had to walk back to Rainham, as few people owned a car in 1948!

Many productions were performed in St Margaret's Hall in Orchard Street (which was demolished in 2001). This presented problems familiar to many amateur theatre groups who do not have a home venue. Access was only allowed to the hall one or two nights before the opening performance and a frantic effort was needed to erect the set before curtain up. Productions usually ended on a Saturday night and the set had to be taken down again by midday the following day, as the hall was used for church activities on Sunday afternoons. These days, setbuilding at the Oasthouse Theatre often begins six or seven weeks before opening night and most rehearsals are able to take place on stage – an undreamt-of luxury for RATS actors in the middle of the twentieth century.

In these early days, the group also took part in festivals around the County. In March 1949, the group performed *In a Glass Darkly* in the Kings Hall, Herne Bay as part of the Kent County Drama Festival. The entrance fee for the festival was 12s 6d. Next, in May 1949, the group entered the Medway Drama Festival organised by The Medway Theatre Guild with the one act play *The Lake of Darkness* by Edward Percy. The author, who was also an MP for Ashford, attended the performance at the Royal Engineers Theatre in Brompton, Gillingham. Other groups taking part included the Irene Weller Players and the Hartlip Amateur Dramatic Society.

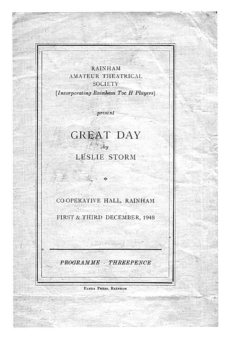

The RATS are born! The programme from our first ever production.

Start of an era. Souvenir programme for opening night.

Later in 1949, the group sought the help of Woodlands School in Gillingham as they were looking for a 14-year-old boy to take part in the play *Queen Elizabeth Slept Here*. The school put forward seven boys for the audition and a lad named Brian Hoare was selected for the part.

The group continued to perform at St Margaret's Hall, but dreamt of having a theatre of their own. At one time, they even built a stage in an old forge in Upchurch. However, it was not deemed viable to open the building to the public because of the remoteness of the location in an age where most people relied on public transport.

At the start of the 1960's, the group was already highly successful and over 1,000 people paid to see the 1962 pantomime (*Jack & the Beanstalk*), including many coachloads from surrounding districts.

Early in 1961, agreement was reached for the group to rehearse in the newly opened Rainham Library. Sadly, this venue was also deemed unsuitable for productions, as the library would not be available to the group until 7pm each evening, which would not have provided adequate time to convert the space into a theatre.

Eager volunteers, led by Fred Haddell and Brian Philpott, set about the task of building a new theatre.

Later that same year, May Hopkins (an original member and Secretary of the group) saw an advertisement in the local paper announcing that part of an Oasthouse in Stratford Lane was for sale – with the suggested use of storage. The advert referred to approximately one third of a building – the portion which was no longer in use as a working oast. Perhaps the association with Stratford, the birthplace of Shakespeare, conjured up ideas because soon members of the RATS were making plans for this empty building and wondering whether their dream of owning their own theatre could become a reality?

The Oasthouse, which was over 100 years old even then, belonged to local landowner and farmer, Jack Clark, who kindly agreed to let the group have the

Members worked into the night to convert the ramshackle building.

building rent free. Under the guidance of Norman Booth, the RATS decided to take the plunge and embark upon the challenge of realising their dream. So began the task of converting this abandoned building into Rainham's very own theatre. To help raise funds, the group held regular jumble sales and continued with their productions in St Margaret's Hall. Monthly subscriptions of 2s.6d also helped to swell the coffers. In addition, patrons could buy a lino-tile for 2s 6d and have their name inscribed on it for posterity!

Whilst the group lacked money, they certainly did not lack enthusiasm. A small band of members, including Brenda Pearson, Zena Haddell and Betty Butcher (ably assisted by junior members of the society), spent most evenings at the unheated Oasthouse cleaning and repairing the building. Whilst male members Brian Philpott and Fred Haddell took charge of the building works, including the construction of a stage and laying new floors. At this stage, Brian tried to get Rainham traders interested in supporting the new theatre either financially or by donating useful items, however the only recorded gift was three sets of crockery.

One thing that the group noticed was that there were no spiders or other creepy crawlies in the building. The process of beer-making involved placing sticks of sulphur onto the hops to eliminate pests and the sulphurous residue ensured that there were no nasty surprises lurking under the debris that had to be cleared away. (The Oasthouse which occupied the other portion of the building continued as a working Oast into the 1970's, and agreement was reached with the owners that they would not lay sulphur until after 10.00 pm on production nights, due to the strong odour which penetrated the dividing wall).

Initially, there were plans for the group to be known as the 'Oasthouse Theatre Club' but, whilst the group were referred to by this name in the early 1960's, they soon became more commonly known as the RATS or the Oasthouse Theatre.

In June 1962, outline planning permission was granted by Gillingham Borough Council to convert the building from a disused silo building into a social centre and theatre. It was full steam ahead! At the AGM later in the year, it was reported that the group had turned a deficit of £23 into a surplus of £36, but that the fund raising must continue to meet the rising renovation costs.

In December 1962, Norman Booth sent a letter to Gillingham Borough Council setting out the society's detailed plans to convert the Oasthouse into a theatre. As the group believed they were going to provide an amenity that Rainham was lacking, they felt that the Borough might like to assist with a small grant. The group had heard that the Council were encouraging the conversion of such Oasthouses, as long as the building was retained in its natural form, to preserve a unique part of the Kentish rural scene. Gillingham Borough Council, in turn, considered approaching Kent County Council for a grant.

The Council's General Purpose Committee discussed the letter on 17 January 1963 and it was decided a sub committee should look into the matter. There was also talk of the Council buying or leasing the building themselves and then, in turn, granting the RaTS a tenancy or sub tenancy. It was at this time that the Oasthouse's owner, Jack Clark, decided to request a weekly rental of £5, at a time when subscriptions for acting membership were £1/16/- per year (that's £1.80 in new money). This minor set back did not deter the members who were eagerly preparing the theatre to open its doors to the public for the first time.

Opening night

After many months of hard work, the theatre was ready for its opening night. Some of the lighting, heating, carpets and even the proscenium arch had come from the Globe Theatre in Chatham and seating from the local Naval Barracks canteen. The main doors were obtained from a picture house in Maidstone before it was demolished.

A specially invited audience witnessed the opening of the Oasthouse Theatre on Friday 8th November 1963. The production was *Billy Liar* by Keith Waterhouse and Willis Hall. Miss Irene Weller performed the opening ceremony and also cut the two tier celebration cake decorated with the traditional theatrical masks of comedy and tragedy. Other invited guests included the Deputy Mayor and Mayoress of Gillingham; Councillor Michael Lewis (still an honorary member today) and his wife; Mr Jack Clark and the Society's President, Mr William Poulton. A Guard of Honour was provided by the Marine Cadets, joined by the Society's officers, Chairman, Norman Booth; Secretary, May Hopkins and Treasurer, Brian Philpott. President William Poulton made a short speech, commenting 'this is one of the proudest days I have had. If you knew how hard members have worked to achieve this..sometimes up until two o'clock in the morning'

A slight dampener, however, was put on the celebrations. Whilst a Theatre Bar had been installed with the help of Truman's Brewery, the society were unable to sell alcohol on the opening night as the licence was still to be approved by the Fire Brigade and local Police.

Dress rehearsal for *Billy Liar*. (from left) Brenda Pearson, Peter Yeman, Christine Crowley, Terry Ray, Annette Allen, Zena Haddell and Norman Booth.

As the curtain opened, a ripple of applause ran through the tiny auditorium marking the achievement of the dream. The first person to appear on the stage was Brenda Pearson who played the part of Florence Boothroyd, Billy's grandmother. Brenda is still playing an active part in the Society as we celebrate our 40th anniversary at the Oasthouse and has now been involved in over 100 productions, having been a member of the group since 1961. In the local press report of the play, Brenda's performance was described as 'a gem of characterization'. Terry Ray took the main role of Billy Fisher whilst Betty Butcher and Les Hopkins played his parents.

However, not all the comments from the press were as encouraging. They also reported that "to generalise on the production, there was a certain amount of over acting by most of the cast and they were evidently plagued by the problem of most amateur groups: that of finding people old enough, or, more often, young enough to look convincing in the parts they were intended to play".

On Saturday 9th November 1963, the general public were admitted to the theatre to witness the first public performance in the 'World's Only Oasthouse Theatre' (a second Oasthouse was converted into a Theatre some years later at Tonbridge, necessitating a change of slogan to 'The World's First Oasthouse Theatre').

The opening night did not go quite as smoothly as planned. Due to the small auditorium and low ceiling it was not possible to have tiered seating. This meant that some of the audience had to resort to tipping up their seats and sitting on the edges in order to be able to see the action. During the interval, Norman Booth apologised and quipped "One answer would be to measure you all when you book your seats!" Instead, however, he promised to raise the last five rows in two six-inch tiers before the pantomime. Otherwise, the evening was a great success and the residents of Rainham were happy to support their newly opened theatre, paying three shillings and ninepence for their tickets and many forking out an extra sixpence for the programme.

Billy Liar was repeated in 1981 to celebrate our 18th birthday and Brenda Pearson was the only member to appear in both productions. This time she changed roles and played Billy's mother.

No sooner had the final curtain fallen on *Billy Liar* than the RATS began preparing for their first pantomime at the Oasthouse, which was to be *Little Red Riding Hood* by Ted Lewis. The production received some favourable reviews from the local press including: "When Rainham Amateur Theatrical Society moved to its new Oasthouse Theatre last year, many supporters wondered if the smaller stage, cramped backstage conditions and dressing room accommodation would lower the high standard of the annual pantomime. But this year's offering proved their fears unfounded!" The group were well on their way to success.

Acquiring the Oasthouse

In February 1964, a cloud appeared on the horizon. All the time and effort put in by members to create the theatre almost came to an abrupt halt when a dispute over land outside the theatre threatened its closure less than six months after the grand opening!

The building firm, Wards Construction Limited, fenced off land outside the theatre which not only caused problems for the RATS, but also local builder Mr Filmer and local farmer Fred Scott, who owned Stratford Farm (on land now occupied by Cherry Tree Close). It meant that people using the lane would have to turn their cars in Mr Filmer's yard.

To add to the problems, Wards Construction removed the theatre's fire escape, which had been erected only a week earlier to comply with local fire regulations, and the society estimated that it would cost £20 to re-instate. This prompted a heated exchange of correspondence between the Society's secretary, Mrs Daphne Philpott, and Wards Construction. The local paper even reported threats of violence (and denials) from both sides as the situation threatened to turn ugly. Eventually, the matter was placed in the hands of local solicitor, Mr Hill.

Productions continued over the following months and finally an amicable agreement was reached, avoiding costly legal action, which could have bankrupted the Society and deprived Rainham of the Theatre which has now been here for 40 years.

It was about this time that discussions reached a head as to whether the council were to buy the building from owner, Jack Clark. Chairman, Norman Booth, had been urging the council to buy the building, as this would facilitate further improvements to the building. The RATS were hoping to take a tenancy or sub tenancy and then sub let part of the building to Toc-H and a local judo club.

In 1964, Gillingham Councillor R.W. Jones announced, "The society is a small body of people doing a very good job. They are working very hard and I think the theatre they are making in the Oasthouse will be an asset to Rainham itself and I think the council should do what it can."

'What it can' turned out to be a grant of £50, because it was in 1964 that the council decided not to buy the Oasthouse, when Jack Clark raised the asking price from £4000 to £6000. This put the RATS in a dilemma and cast yet more doubt on their future. An internal memo in 1964 enquired whether Jack Clark would accept £3000 cash for the building and so began a round of discussions and negotiations. In the interim period, the group decided to continue with the tenancy and a figure of £6 6s per week was agreed, with a view to possibly purchasing the building over a 10-year period.

In March 1965, the group were reluctant to pay the rent as they felt the building needed too much attention and repair. In a letter to Frank Hill & Co Solicitors in September 1965, the society's secretary wrote "the uncertainty of our occupation and the condition of the building makes us rather apprehensive about the future."

At this stage, Jack Clark offered the building to the group for £4000 plus back rent for the past four years, which totalled an additional £1040. However, the members were not happy about the back rent, as a rent-free period had originally been agreed.

But it seemed the RATS were left with little alternative if they wished to remain in the Oasthouse, where members had spent many hours creating the charming theatre that was now becoming popular with local residents. Mr Clark's solicitors decided to force the issue by warning "if the matter cannot be finally settled to Mr Clarks satisfaction, he will take drastic measures!" The drastic measures he had in mind were apparently to fit padlocks to the main doors to exclude members from the premises!

Facing the possibility of seeing all their hard work go to waste, the determined pioneers of the Rainham Amateur Theatrical Society took the momentous decision to buy the building themselves and agreed to pay £4800 for the Oasthouse over a period of 16 years. They then set about securing a mortgage on the property and the first repayment of £25 was made on 1 October 1966. At last the RATS had a Theatre of our own.

Events & Special Occasions

The gusto and enthusiasm that the original members had shown in the early days also manifested itself in the 'extra curricular' activities organised by the executive committee. When the Oasthouse first opened its doors to the public, the annual dinner and dance was a very formal affair and dinner was always six or seven courses at a prestigious local venue with members expected to dress up in black tie attire. Minutes of early committee meetings show that the menu for these occasions was often discussed at great length, but it appears to have been worth it as the dinner and dance was always well attended. The first dinner and dance was held in 1963 at The Sun Hotel in Chatham and was attended by 60 members. The following year, the venue was the Central Hotel in Featherby Road, Gillingham. It is a sign of the remarkable endurance of the Oasthouse Theatre that the Central Hotel became The Avenue Nightclub, then Bar Rio and has now been demolished to make way for a housing development. The venues for subsequent dances have been many and varied, including; Sittingbourne Town Hall, The Coniston Hotel, Boxley Country Club, The Roffen Club, The Beacon Court and The Hastings Arms. Support for these functions has decreased in latter years and our annual dinner and dance is a thing of the past.

Other social events, however, have gone from strength to strength and have reflected changing fashions over the years. Regular Friday night bingo was popular for over four years in the 1970's and, in the early 1990's, Wine & Wisdom evenings were introduced and they remain as popular as ever today.

Over the years, social events have played a significant part in the life of the society by encouraging members to maintain contact outside of play runs, whilst at the same time raising much needed funds for the upkeep of the building. Many fund raising activities have been arranged over the years, including sponsored events, carnivals, jumble sales, boot fairs and even Tupperware parties! Car rallies were popular at one stage, but perhaps the rule that the winner had to organise the next car rally hastened their demise.

The RaTS are proud to have raised money over the years for various charities. The Club Room housed a full sized ping-pong table during the 1970's and two table tennis marathons were held which raised over £300 towards the purchase of a special hospital bed. Years later, RATS stalwart Brenda Pearson spent a few nights in hospital and found herself lying opposite the bed, which bore a plaque thanking the RATS for their contribution (her demands to be moved to "her" bed apparently fell on deaf ears!).

Two of the most memorable fund-raising events were the twenty-four hour 'pantothons'. *Dick Whittington* in 1987 and *Babes in the Wood* in 1990 were performed a total of 9 times each from midday Saturday to midday Sunday, raising funds for the NSPCC and the Invicta Appeal for the Disabled, as well as a contribu-

The RATS football team (left) struggled to a 5-5 draw with the Folk Club. From left: Nigel Medhurst, David O'Brien, Mike Mullinger, Steve Berry, Alex Bushell, Steve Harbour, Jon Hammell, Dean Caston, Chris Williams, Steve Hewlett and Bill Beck, with linesmen Peter O'Brien and Jeffrey Marsh.

1960's productions were celebrated with a fish & chip supper in the auditorium.

tion to the Oasthouse Building Fund. The casts of both pantomimes even swapped roles in the early hours of the morning to add a bit of variety and some 'guest performers' took part to give cast members the chance of a couple of hours sleep in the middle of the night. The casts were supported by dedicated backstage and tea bar crews, not to mention the audiences who were with them throughout the night, ensuring that audience participation was always possible (one person sat through six night-time performances – either he suffered from insomnia or had been thrown out by his wife). Any flagging spirits among the cast were kept alive by the provision of casseroles, cornflakes, a full cooked breakfast and the prospect of a champagne reception with the Mayor, which took place after the final performance of *Babes in the Wood*.

Bill and Joy Garlick ran the folk club for some years and they were instrumental in organising a friendly football match between the Folk Club and Theatre members in 1984. The match finished as a 5 - 5 draw with Mike Mullinger (RATS) and Bill Vandone (Folk) as players of the match. Referee was non–member George Barwick and linesmen were Jeffrey Marsh and Peter O'Brien. RATS lovelies Hazel O'Brien, Julie Miskimmin and Melody Harbour supplied the cheerleading.

Another tradition which grew up at the Oasthouse Theatre was 'Potted Pantomimes'. Up until the late 1990's, these were the highlight of the last night of the annual pantomime. They were introduced in 1969 after Brenda Pearson failed to secure a part in the annual pantomime and so decided to write her own. This was rehearsed with other disappointed members and performed to the main cast after the last night. In the early years, potted pantos had proper scripts that were written independently of the main pantomime and had to be read and approved by the Theatre Committee. The 'potted' cast had proper rehearsals and a rather polished satire was the result. As the years passed, scripts became rather risqué and the cast was made up of backstage crew, front of house staff and audience members. Hurried rehearsals took place in between the matinee shows on Saturdays – so nearly all the cast would go on with a script! The 'potted panto' cast would use the costumes from the main pantomime and would lampoon characters and situations from the main pantomime. As the tradition grew, the cast of the main pantomime would feel rather 'put out' if they weren't mentioned! Lack of backstage crew, and less time in between matinee shows has seen the demise of this institution, but many who witnessed them retain fond memories of the Potted Panto.

The after-show party is one tradition which has endured, although this has become more of a time to unwind than to party now! In the late 1960's, the traditional after- show celebration was a fish and chip supper (out of the paper) enjoyed in the auditorium! During the 1970's and 80's, a disco was held on the stage after the last performance of each show and, as the last-night audience consisted mainly of the cast's family and friends, they were always well received. Changes in people's tastes meant that the discos were discontinued, but the social gatherings continue – as does the tradition of the director buying a round of drinks for cast and backstage crew, while the cast contribute to a present for the director, often providing a treasured souvenir of the production.

Bert and Mercia Read enter into the spirit of potted panto as the oldest Babes in the Wood on record, complete with zimmer frame.

A toast to the RATS mascot to celebrate the first 10 years at the theatre. (From left) Brenda Pearson, Betty Butcher, Fred Haddell, Jack Butcher, Zena Haddell, Ruth Banham and chairman, Bill Banham.

The RaTS enjoy celebrating the landmark years in the society's history and have held parties for various anniversaries. There were no celebrations actually recorded for the 10th anniversary of the opening of the Oasthouse, although original members toasted the RATS mascot and a photograph depicting the occasion still resides in the theatre. For the 18th anniversary of the opening of the theatre, *Billy Liar* (the first play performed at the Oast) was performed again (see memorable productions). The 50th anniversary celebrations of the creation of the Rainham Amateur Theatrical Society were in 1998 and a party, attended by members past and present, was held at The Walnut Tree Club, Gillingham. In May 1992, founder members of the RATS were invited to a reunion party at the Oasthouse Theatre. Hetty Elcombe, Min Woolley, Violet Wall & Annetta Newell were among cast members from the RATS first ever production, *Great Day* by Leslie Storm (1948), who attended a special gala matinee performance of *All for your Delight*.

A rather large miscalculation of dates was made when we celebrated 25 years at the Oasthouse one year too early in 1987! A great amount of preparation went in to selecting plays to perform that year. A survey was circulated to all the members asking them which plays from the past 25 years they would like to see staged again and a whole year's programme was agreed with repeat runs of the five most popular plays seen at the Oasthouse. When someone then pointed out that, as the official opening of the Oasthouse Theatre was in November 1963, we shouldn't be celebrating the 25th anniversary until 1988, it was decided that too much planning had taken place to let a small detail like the facts get in the way of a good party. So the plays were performed (and enjoyed by audiences), the celebrations went ahead, including full press publicity, and no one was any the wiser (until now!).

"Any excuse for a celebration" could be the RATS motto, as the Queens Silver and Golden Jubilees featured quite heavily in the RATS programmes for 1977 and 2002. In 1977, *This Happy Breed* was selected in a competition to choose the 'Play of the Reign' and was performed at the Oasthouse Theatre to rave reviews. In 2002 and 2003, various events were organised in and around the Oasthouse to celebrate the Queen's Golden Jubilee and the 50th anniversary of her actual Coronation. Celebration concerts were held in nearby St Margaret's Church, which raised funds for both the Oasthouse and the Church roof fund. Dean Caston also organised a pageant along the streets of Rainham and hundreds of people lined the pavements to cheer the parade on.

Landmark occasions for members have also been celebrated. In 1973, RATS stalwart Christine Crowley moved out of the area and a 'This is your Life' evening was arranged. Several members participated and Christine was given a great send-off. In June 1986, a surprise party was organised in honour of Brenda Pearson's 25 years service to the RATS. Pauline Harley collected Brenda to take her to the theatre on the pretext of attending a barbeque and, when they stopped off on the way, Pauline rang on ahead to warn the partygoers that Brenda was on her way. When she arrived, Brenda was so overwhelmed that she stepped under the welcome banner and had to go outside and come in again to charge through the banner, whilst being cheered on by members past and present. 25th anniversary

Greg Pexton, Robin Clark and Mike Mullinger morris-dance their way to laughs in *Just The Ticket* (1981). (See Memorable Productions page 58)

presentations have also been made to Keith Sheepwash, Val Warn & Melody Harbour.

In 1965, several members took part as 'extras' in the filming of a BBC documentary *The War Game*. Peter Watkins, the producer, wrote several letters to advise of the date the programme would be aired. Unfortunately, due to the contentious subject matter, the programme was never broadcast, so the members involved didn't get (in the words of Andy Warhol) their '15 minutes of fame' on this occasion!

To celebrate our 40th anniversary at the Oasthouse, in addition to producing this book, the RaTS decided to revive a home-grown musical (*The Smuggler and the Lady*) and to return to one of our earliest traditions by holding a dinner and dance at Gillingham Golf Club, just along the road from the old Central Hotel (see 75th anniversary book for details of how this went!).

What the Papers say

Most professional actors keep a scrapbook or folder of press cuttings; at least until they become so famous that the task becomes too time-consuming. Many amateur actors do the same. However much we claim to do it for the art, any actor dreams occasionally of seeing their name in lights and a photo or mention in the local paper always brings a frisson of pleasure. An equal measure of disappointment accompanies the discovery that the editor's desire to cut 20 words from the review to make it fit the page, means that our own name ends up in the newsroom waste bin. Occasionally a local 'drama critic' takes their role so seriously that they become too frank for comfort in their criticism and we pretend that the newsagent had sold out of the paper when we finally remembered to go to the shop.

In the long run, however, local theatre groups rely on the local press for much needed publicity and the local press rely on local activities such as theatre to fill their papers. A mutually beneficial relationship exists and press cuttings provide an interesting contribution to our Oasthouse Theatre archive.

Press opinions on one of the earliest productions at the Oasthouse Theatre, *The Crooked Tree* in 1964, illustrate just how subjective these reports can be. One critic, identified only as I.G.D. (reviewers often signed off with just their initials), began his report "I came away from the RATS Theatre Club presentation of *The Crooked Tree* by T.B. Morris feeling that perhaps this was not one of the RATS more outstanding productions" and went on to criticise the story (using a quotation from the play) as "too damn silly and melodramatic". The report appeared under the strapline "This Crooked Tree nearly toppled". In a rival newspaper, a different perspective was given under the headline "Rapture over RATS". The reviewer, identified as M.H., advised that "visitors to Rainham's Oasthouse Theatre can look out for a bright new approach to drama".

Although records do not indicate who M.H actually was, it is safe to assume that he was a male, as he went on to observe "The cast consisted wholly of women, and frankly this idea, plus the fact that they were being directed by a woman, produced strong misgivings as, most times, women in large doses can be such a bore". One can only imagine the outraged response that such a comment would provoke today. However, M.H. was not alone in making what could be termed 'politically incorrect' observations. The following year, a reporter identified as S.A. visited the Oasthouse to watch *Women of Twilight*, a play set in a home for unmarried mothers, and was moved to note that it was not surprising that the cast seemed to enjoy themselves as "there can be few women who do not like to revel in a little sluttishness now and then". Perhaps it is just as well that they stuck to their initials.

J.N.B. redressed the balance somewhat in 1967 after watching *The Two Mrs Carrolls*. Under the banner "RATS men were no match for brilliant ladies" he (or perhaps she) wrote "some of the ladies carry through their part with a distinctly

Brenda Pearson and Joe Harley, described by Duncan Rand as "like a mettlesome pair-in-hand", *Sleeping Beauty* 1974.

professional flourish – but there seems to be a lack of budding promise among most of the men".

The 1960's, however, were mainly characterised by fulsome praise for the RATS productions and critics were usually ready to overlook minor imperfections, as in one review of our 1969 pantomime, *Jack and the Beanstalk*: "There were one or two imperfections, of course, in the memory of lines and in curtains opening at the wrong time, but much more important was the zestful sense of fun which is infectious in the Oasthouse and makes the blemishes easily forgivable".

Later in 1969, one blemish (in Agatha Christie's *The Hollow*) was not so easily forgiven. Under the grand banner of 'Jeremy Gates at the Theatre', the reviewer observed "Chris Williams makes a fine job of Cristow, until the time comes for him to be murdered ..... he dies in a scene straight out of 'Carry on Bonehead'. He grips his stomach when he's been shot in the mouth, and his contortions in the throes of death bring Act 1 to a side-splitting finale".

In the early 1970's, two major figures in the local amateur theatre scene were writing for the main local newspapers – Jimmy Hodge, who is still reviewing our plays as we celebrate 40 years at the Oasthouse, and Duncan Rand, whose use of language in the Evening Post's 'On Stage' column was almost poetic. In his review of *Sleeping Beauty* in 1974, he felt that the comedy duo had held the show together, commenting, "Joseph Harley and Brenda Pearson – like a mettlesome pair-in-hand – plunging and tossing, towed the whole vehicle (somewhat creaky

20

Jimmy Hodge, the greatest Medway theatre journalist of the past 40 years.

here and there) with indefatigable vigour". This flowery language could sometimes soften the impact of a harsher observation. His review of *Sleeping Beauty* continued "Here and there, a sense of vigorous improvisation could have been replaced profitably by greater precision in vocal and visual effect". In other words, 'less ad-libbing would have helped'!

Whatever the critics thought, RATS audiences continued to enjoy our productions and occasionally felt moved to set the record straight, as when F. Horgan (after reading a review of our 1975 production of *Ladies of Spirit*) wrote to the Chatham, Rochester and Gillingham News Showpage: "The RATS are amateurs and, to my mind, most of their shows surpass London shows. They give up a lot of their time and all work hard to put on these plays and I think it poor taste to belittle their efforts". Hear, Hear!

However, criticism was soon to reach new heights. In the mid 1970's, The Evening Post employed a 'drama critic' who struck terror into the hearts of amateur players throughout the Medway Towns. His name was Kieron Wood and he seemed to feel that it was his mission in his regular 'On Stage' column to point out the shortcomings of anyone who dared to tread the amateur boards. Take this example, from his review of our 1976 production of *Deadly Record*: "A mediocre performance is bad enough when the play is outstanding. When the play is mediocre too, it can be positively second-rate. The trouble with *Deadly Record*, at the Rainham Oasthouse Theatre, was that the actors and backstage workers seemed to be happy with far less than perfection in a play which was improbable and long-winded to start with." He went on to pronounce that "Props were a little slapdash, with no division or number on the policeman's uniform, sticking exit doors and odd loudspeaker noises, and black marks to almost everyone for taking far too many prompts." As Basil Fawlty once said: "Otherwise OK?".

Neither was Kieron a great fan of our pantomimes. In 1976, our panto, *Ali Baba*, was struck by an outbreak of flu among 3 cast members. Mr Wood was unsympathetic: "Without wanting to be unkind, it might have been better for the reputation of amateur dramatics if the whole cast had been struck down before the opening night. A truly tedious script, makeshift costumes, poor acting and an utter lack of any sustained contact with the audience made *Ali Baba* one of the most disappointing pantos of the season." It makes one wonder what he said about THE most disappointing panto of the season! He even went so far as to criticise the audience "whose response to jokes and songs was desultory." Two years later, *Red Riding Hood* didn't fare any better: "Casting problems and a dreary script combined to make *Red Riding Hood* a big let-down at the Rainham Oasthouse Theatre. Lighting was tardy, scenery lacked atmosphere and the choreography suffered from the same old problems – unlikely fairies with furrowed brows and looks of rapt concentration studying the other dancers to see they didn't get out of step."

He wasn't impossible to impress, however, and we struck lucky with *Strike Happy* when he wrote: "The production started slowly but built up into a riot of amorous misunderstandings and slapstick humour. A couple of the cast seemed at a loose end as to what to do with their hands, but the audience had no such problems. Their applause marked what seems to be an upturn in the standards of this talented group."

In July 1978, the 'On Stage' column was taken over by Neil Clements and the Medway drama community breathed a collective sigh of relief.

Coverage in the Chatham, Rochester & Gillingham News during the 1970's was much more friendly, with staunch amateur theatre supporter, Jimmy Hodge, leading the way with his weekly feature 'Keeping Tabs'. The JIMI Awards (see Festivals and Awards chapter) provided a happy annual boost to amateurs involved in Medway theatre and his reviews also provided encouragement. For example, his 1978 review of *Bonaventure*, set in a convent, began: "Rainham Amateur Theatrical Society has always had fine leading performers. And the RATS performance of *Bonaventure* by Charlotte Hastings is no exception. Grace Murrell, in the title role, is a graceful personality and neatly carries the Sister's habit. But she also displays fire and determination in her bid to uncover the truth. The same compliments can be paid to the experienced Rita Saunders as the whirlwind cook whose robes swish mightily when she gets her Irish up!" A fitting tribute to Rita, one of the Oasthouse founder members, who retired from the Oasthouse stage after this performance.

Other writers for 'The News' were equally positive about our efforts. In 1977 Anne Briggs wrote "It is rare for a play by an amateur group to be so engrossing that more than two hours pass unnoticed and so well performed that the end of the interval cannot come fast enough. But I am sure I was not alone in finding this the case with Rainham Amateur Theatrical Society's production of Michael Pertwee's *Night Was our Friend*. Much of the credit goes to Peter O'Brien, whose performance was not far short of outstanding." And remember *Ali Baba*? ("one of the most disappointing pantos of the season") – Christine Wood disagreed with Kieron Wood, writing "Full of Eastern promise – that's the verdict on the first night of Rainham Amateur Theatrical Society's pantomime *Ali Baba & the 40 Thieves*. And if the RATS can keep up the same verve and enthusiasm for the rest of the run, they will be onto a winner."

By the mid 1980's, the 'On Stage' banner for the Evening Post was being carried by Elaine Jones, who appeared to draw on the Kieron Wood Critic's Handbook when she reviewed *The Creature Creeps* in 1985: "While The Creature Crept all over the stage at Rainham's Oasthouse Theatre, this reporter was wishing there was some way I could have crept out. Unfortunately there was more than one of those desperate cringe-making moments when the whole team lost the thread completely."

At 'The News', Jimmy Hodge was still 'Keeping Tabs' and was much impressed with a stripping scene by Julie Miskimmin in *Lock Up Your Daughters* in 1985: "each garment was removed with the skill of a professional stripper" and he felt that this scene "made the night out worthwhile" – so much so that Julie, along with Peter O'Brien, won 2 of the last ever JIMI Awards for this production.

Sophie Williams was also providing support from the Chatham News stable in the 80s. She wrote of *The Gentle Hook* in 1986: "There was no doubt in the audience's mind about the standard of the performance and their enjoyment of the mystery – both were high." However Sophie was not always quite so impressed and, whilst generally praising *Deathtrap*, she noted "The production failed to fully exploit the melodrama of the moment when Clifford apparently returns from the grave and beats Sydney to death. The club looked like a leftover from It's a Knockout and Clifford looked a little too healthy for a recently garrotted man."

When the press come to visit during panto season, it is always good to work a mention into the jokes. Melody Foreman (the late 1980's guardian of the 'On Stage' column) certainly appreciated the namedropping during *Jack & the Beanstalk* which she wrote "was full of colour with slapstick comedy thrust upon the audience throughout the show." Later in the review she reveals "Scene Two – outside the palace – stuck in my mind after Eustace Clotworthy (played by Dean Caston) announced to Poppy 'I'm the palace herald'. The comical dame replied 'I don't care if you're the Evening Post.'"

The 1990's saw a tendency towards guest reviewers in the local papers. In 1992, professional actor John Solomon Clarke reviewed *Look Who's Talking* for the Chatham News. He was impressed with his welcome: "At a time when professional theatres are going dark all over the country, it was a joy to experience the welcoming atmosphere of this highly successful theatre, an object lesson for any theatres experiencing membership problems." He was impressed with the show: "Pace, pitch and power were all there. This could have been any professional 'rep' treating a first night full house to two hours of excellent entertainment." And he was most impressed with actor Mike Newvell: "The beautifully understated ease which demonstrates the pro's capacity to make acting look easy, combined with superb timing and comic sense, wholly captured my admiration. This performance was simply professional."

The cast of Lord Arthur Savile's Crime show "how it should be done". From left standing: Mark Sanders, Steve Berry, Jack Homewood, Colin Mepstead, Sue Munn and Pat Sanders, seated: Kathy West, Jeni Boyns, Brenda Pearson and Helen Caston.

Another guest reviewer, David Spiers, became a regular visitor to the Oasthouse. Writing under the name Dave Hawes, he reviewed many productions around the turn of the 21st century and was usually impressed with what he saw, as in the case of *Dead Easy* in March 2001: "*Dead Easy* was more than just the title of the play: it was dead easy to feel relaxed and comfortable with the quartet of high-flying businessmen, played by Colin Mepstead, Max Thompson, Andy Harding and Pat Sanders, all giving a laid-back and untheatrically refreshing style of acting, the hallmark of Rainham Theatrical Society actors".

A chapter concerning reviews of our productions would not be complete without an honourable mention for Olga Laramann. Olga has, for many years, been our regional representative at the National Operatic and Dramatic Society (NODA) and has been attending productions at the Oasthouse (and many other theatres) for longer than she cares to remember. Olga contributes a review of each show to the NODA magazine and appreciates that amateur actors want to see their name mentioned and far prefer to read something nice about themselves. She is unstintingly kind and her most extreme criticism tends to be 'interesting' as in "A most interesting and entertaining production came from the RATS when they presented this story of murder and mayhem set within a large department store" (*Counter Crime* July 1988). More typical is the comment "An exciting and at

Val Warn proudly shows off the theatre box office, where her smiling face has greeted audiences for many years.

times also very amusing production, and the whole cast are to be congratulated" (*Local Murder* 1989).

The last word, however, should go to the greatest Medway theatre critic, Jimmy Hodge. Now writing for the Medway Messenger (successor to the Evening Post), Jimmy reviewed our July 2003 production and confirms the continuing high standard of our shows: "There are a number of framed certificates in the foyer of the Oasthouse Theatre in Rainham, all awarded for excellence in various drama competitions over the years. The RaTS deserve another one for their latest production, *Lord Arthur Savile's Crime*, a period drama ..... Some amateur producers in Medway ought to catch up with this offering, if only to see how it should be done".

Whether good, bad or indifferent, the Oasthouse Theatre thanks all those who have provided publicity by covering our activities in various publications over the years. As the old saying goes "There's only one thing worse than being written about – and that's NOT being written about".

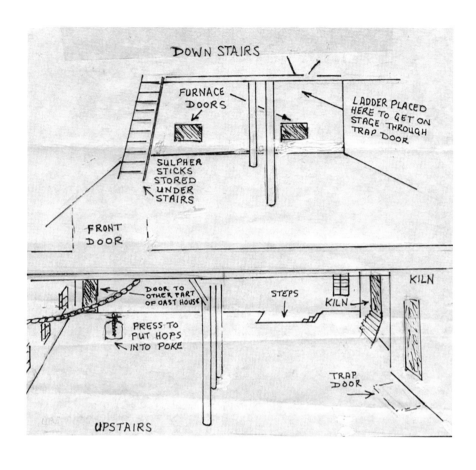

A drawing by Brenda Pearson depicting the Oasthouse as it was prior to conversion.

Changes to the Building

In the 40 years since the Oasthouse Theatre first opened its doors to the public, many changes have taken place to the building. Some changes have been made to improve conditions for actors and backstage crew, some changes have made life more comfortable for the audience and some changes have been necessary to ensure the safety of all who use the theatre. Whatever the reason, the work has required dedication and commitment from the founder members and those who have taken up the baton in the intervening four decades.

Let us take an imaginary tour of the Oasthouse Theatre to chronicle the changes.

Entrance, Foyer & Bar

The entrance to the Theatre has always been from Stratford Lane. The original doors were wooden and were replaced by the more secure steel ones we have today after a break-in in 1976. In May 1964, it was suggested that the floor to the entrance hall should be tiled and that members and visitors should be encouraged to "buy a tile". It was intended to display a plan of the tiles on the foyer wall showing the donors details. It is not recorded how much money (if any) was collected for this project, but the tiling was never put in place and the floor has remained untiled to this day.

The foyer, and indeed the whole of the ground floor, was carpeted in 1976. Bill Banham, who was Chairman at the time, saw an advertisement for Hardy's of Gravesend, who were selling their showroom carpet and the committee decided to purchase it. Up until 1976, the 'carpet' was rather patchy (not to mention dangerous) as it consisted of a collection of off-cuts and rugs arranged over the floor. In the 1990's, the committee decided that the Hardy's carpet was showing signs of wear and tear and agreed to have the entire theatre re-carpeted, using the services of Twydall Carpets.

In 1974, Bill Banham came up with a novel fund raising idea. He had a number of small wooden shields made and these were sold to members, who could have their name added before the shield was fixed to the wall of the theatre bar and foyer for posterity. When professional sign-writer Bill Garlick joined the Theatre a couple of years later, he took over the design of the shields. As time went by, the shields became more intricate with various crests and images added by special request. For a number of years, this was the most striking feature of the bar area until, in 1980, it was decided that there were really too many shields and they were removed during a redecoration of the foyer area.

The original method of gaining access to the upper floor (as with most Oasthouses) was by clambering up a steep set of open tread stairs. These were considered unsuitable for members of the public and a new staircase was installed in 1962, with assistance from Mr House of the Wool Shop in Rainham. This

The theatre stairlift claims its only victim!

staircase, too, was rather steep and it was replaced in the early 1970's by the staircase which takes you upstairs to the auditorium today. In July 1994, we performed a thriller called *Deadlock*, which required a working stairlift to be installed on stage, in order that a character called Victor Fleming could meet his demise through electrocution by stairlift. As several of our more senior patrons were finding the theatre stairs difficult to manage, we decided to kill two birds with one stone (excuse the pun) by contracting a company to install a stairlift on stage and then transfer it to the real stairs at the end of the production. Thanks to regular servicing, the stairlift is still going strong and fortunately Victor Fleming remains its only victim!

As we continue our tour of the lower floor, we come to what is now the bar area. When the building first opened its doors to the public, the foyer floor sloped away from the door so the current bar area (which was unused at that stage) was more than two feet lower than it is now. The bar was originally upstairs, which caused problems of noise on rehearsal and performance nights. So, in 1971, it was proposed by the committee to relocate the theatre bar to a more appropriate space on the ground floor. Brenda Pearson made a scale model of the proposal but it wasn't until 5 years later, in 1976, that the new bar was completed and opened for business. The bar has been refurbished several times since then and recently a large refrigeration unit has been installed. A store area, boiler room and office were erected behind the bar in 1989 at a cost of £3418. The floor had to be raised in line with the bar and club room to allow easy access to all the rooms without too many slopes or steps, particularly for the barrels of beer that had to be transported from the front door! In 2002, the RaTS AGM voted to make the building a no

Outside

The access lane to the theatre was a dirt track for many years and the 'car park' (which had reputedly housed another Oasthouse which burnt down) was a small patch of waste ground opposite the main doors. In 1981, Hidsons of Rainham made a successful bid to purchase the land and convert it to a concrete car park as an extension to their existing one (at £20,000 it was a bit out of our price range!). Hidsons very generously installed a gate for access from the lane for members and patrons to use the car park in the evenings.

The other portion of our Oasthouse was a working oast until the mid 1970's, when it fell into disrepair and was used for activities such as football practice for a local boys team. The conversion of this part of the building into residential flats created potential access problems, when the builders drew up plans which gave no vehicular access at all to the theatre. The plans included fencing off the entrance to the Oasthouse Theatre and constructing steps up to it. In 1988 Chairman, Keith Sheepwash, and Treasurer, Val Warn, spent many hours negotiating with Mr Flaherty (the builder who was converting the adjacent section into flats) and his surveyor about the land outside the theatre. They agreed that when the lane was altered, it would not affect the access to the theatre. However, when members came to the theatre one evening they found a two-foot drop outside the main doors. After further lengthy negotiations, the builders agreed to make a slope enabling us to gain access to the theatre. The black railing outside the theatre is a permanent reminder of the drop that would have been left had Keith and Val not used their influencing skills!

In more recent years, due to increased vandalism to cars parked overnight, Hidsons have erected secure fencing around the original car park. However, they still permit theatre members and patrons the use of their main car park in the evenings.

Miscellaneous

Various smaller, but often expensive, changes have had to be made to the building due to the increased legal requirements for health & safety. Fire doors have had to be fitted or upgraded and smoke alarms installed. The renewal of the theatres bar licence depended on us fitting a smoke detection system at a cost of over £3K and the licence was held back for some weeks in 1996 until this was installed. Fire doors had to be fitted to both the kilns as the existing ones were not sufficient and safety windows had to be installed in the clubroom door and the door to the corridor.

Over the years the essential changes we have made to the building have probably changed its appearance beyond recognition for the small band of members who started it all in 1962. One feature, however, remains constant - the commitment and dedication of each new generation of RaTS members.

Earl Street,
Maidstone, Kent
Box Office
Telephone
Maidstone 758611

FINALS WEEK

KENT FULL LENGTH PLAY FESTIVAL 1992

TUESDAY 9th JUNE 7.45 pm

Messiah by Martin Sherman

presented by **FOLKESTONE OPERATIC & DRAMATIC SOCIETY**

THURSDAY 11th JUNE 7.45 pm

Was He Anyone? by N.F. Simpson

presented by **TENTERDEN OPERATIC & DRAMATIC SOCIETY**

SATURDAY 13th JUNE 7.30 pm

The March on Russia by David Storey

presented by

RAINHAM AMATEUR THEATRICAL SOCIETY

To be adjudicated by **Mr. Kenneth Pickering M.A. Ph.D.**
Presentation of Awards for the Preliminary Round of the Festival
will be made after the Saturday performance by
Mrs. Brenda Trench
Chairman, Kent County Council

Tickets **£4.00 TUESDAY** and **THURSDAY**
£4.50 SATURDAY
Available from **Hazlitt Theatre Box Office,**
Earl Street, Maidstone. Tel: 758611

34

Festivals & Awards

Over the years, the RaTS have taken part in many drama festivals which, as well as raising the profile of the theatre, gives an added edge to productions. Competing against other groups is a good learning experience and can be both rewarding and stressful. The adjudicators' remarks are sometimes not as glowing as the actors would like but, in that situation, it is always wise to remember that it is only one person's opinion.

Kent Drama

The Kent Drama Awards are open to all amateur theatre groups in Kent to enter a full-length play with a cast of three or more actors. The RATS first recorded entry in the full-length play festival was *Ten Little Niggers* by Agatha Christie in March 1983 and our first award was won by Peter O'Brien, who earned the Irene Weller Award for Special Achievement for his performance as Cooper in *A Month of Sundays* in 1991.

All groups first performed plays in their own premises. The adjudicator would award a score for various aspects of the production such as presentation, production and acting. The three highest scoring plays would then have to transport their set, props and costumes to The Hazlitt Theatre in Maidstone for the finals, the three plays being staged on Tuesday, Thursday and Saturday of one week. A new adjudicator was always drafted in to judge the top three and the winners would be announced after the last play on the Saturday. Moving the production to another location meant a gargantuan effort by everyone involved, particularly the stage crew.

The RaTS have reached the finals twice, in 1992 with "The March on Russia" when they were placed 2nd and 1993 with "The Diary of Anne Frank" which earned 3rd place. Both of these productions were directed by Chris Williams, who took commitment to festival success to new levels. As The Hazlitt Theatre is more than four times the size of the Oasthouse, extra rehearsals were scheduled to ensure the actors could practise projecting their voices. The set was erected in the car park outside the oasthouse as a practice run for the stage crew, who had to be able to assemble and strike the set quickly (a skill lost in the passage of time since our days in St Margaret's Hall). The actors then rehearsed in the large open space.

Dwindling support for this festival, possibly due to the cost and time needed to transport an entire set to Maidstone, led to its demise in the late 1990's. However, it was re-vamped in 2000 with a new title "The On Stage in Kent Awards" (OSKA's!) and the awards are now presented at a gala dinner at prestigious venues. The re-named festival saw two of our members nominated for awards for their performances in *The Vigil* in 2000; Jean Russell for 'Best Actress' and David O'Brien for 'Best Actor' which he went on to win. Brenda Pearson received a nomination in 2001 for 'Best Actress' in *Dead Easy*.

The cast of *The Diary of Anne Frank* pose outside The Hazlitt Theatre, Maidstone, before finals night.

Peter Gray (left) and Peter O'Brien while away the hours in *A Month of Sundays*, 1991.

Extra thought, effort and attention to detail often goes in to festival plays. Although all plays require the same commitment and professionalism, the festivals often bring out the competitive side in everyone involved. In *Quiet Affairs* by Tony Onwin in 1994, Steve Berry attended Thanet Technical College (former students include TV chef Gary Rhodes) for two days to learn the basics of Silver Service for his role as the waiter in a high-class restaurant.

The Kent Drama One–Act Festival is no longer around, but we have on more than one occasion hosted part of this festival. In 1984, The Tunstall Players performed in the festival with *Henry Hereafter* at the Oast and our entry was *Bang, You're Dead* (although the programme billed it as *Bang Your Dead*, which would have been a different play altogether). In 1991, The Wallace Collection visited the Oasthouse with their entry *The Harpy and the Slob* and we performed *Shadows*. Rena Pope adjudicated the 1991 festival in which we were placed 8th and we received some constructive feedback from her for our production.

Duncan Rand

Duncan Rand was a local journalist and drama adjudicator as well as being one-time chairman of Medway Little Theatre Club. He had the idea for a drama festival in 1973, not only to bring drama groups together but also to provide access to a theatre for groups who generally performed in halls or other venues. The one-act festival, now named in his honour, is still going strong today and is held annually at Rochester's Medway Little Theatre. The RaTS have entered this festival many times in the past but, as it now clashes with our own production, we have been unable to spare any actors or backstage staff in more recent years. Our many entries in this festival include *The Day the Flame Went Out* in 1977, a home written play by member Gill Ryder and for which Bill Beck received a highly commended certificate; *Bang You're Dead* in 1984; *Can You Hear the Music* and *Sparrows* in 1990 for which Brian Eratt was awarded 'Best Actor'. The Youth Group have also entered many times in the past and have been very successful with many awards including Jeni Boyns achieving 'Best Actress' in 1998.

Other festivals that have come and gone include the Medway Drama Festival in the 1960's and the Kent County Drama Festival in which we performed *In a Glass Darkly* in 1949 at The Kings Hall, Herne Bay.

JIMI's

Another competition in which the group strived for success was the 'JIMI' awards. These were initiated and adjudicated by Jimmy Hodge, local newspaper theatre correspondent, in 1970 to mark the achievements of the area's top performers. Jimmy was then the show business editor of the Chatham, Rochester & Gillingham News. He watched every single production in the Medway Towns between 1970 and 1986 and held an annual awards ceremony at various local venues. Certificates and engraved trophies were presented to people from all walks of theatre life including musicals, variety, drama, comedy and even backstage and directors.

Another award won by the RATS.

Oasthouse Theatre productions have earned several 'JIMI' awards over the years. In 1974, Brenda Pearson won Drama Producer of the Year for *Bang, You're Dead*, Steve Harbour was awarded Stage Manager of the Year in 1977 for *This Happy Breed* – a production which also earned a JIMI for director, Peter O'Brien. The following year, Kay Jones won Most Promising Newcomer for her role in *Bonaventure* and, in 1985, Peter O'Brien won Best Actor and Julie Miskimmin Best Actress for *Lock up Your Daughters*. Janet May (later Janet Wyatt) won Best Variety Actress for our 1980 pantomime, *The Wizard who Wasn't*.

In 1986 as a 'thank-you' for his services to local amateur theatre, representatives from all the local groups attended a 'This is Your Life' evening for Jimmy hosted by the RATS at the Oasthouse. Jimmy moved on to teach journalism and has recently returned to his roots to cover local productions as a freelance journalist.

Top Town

In 1966, RATS entered the Top Town Challenge Week at Maidstone's Municipal Theatre and became the first group from Medway to win the competition. This was all the more remarkable as it was the first time we had entered. Our potted version of the hit show *Merry Switzerland*, appears to have particularly impressed the judges with its originality. Betty Butcher also said at the time "We also won points because we managed not to overstay our welcome. We started and finished right on time".

Jimmy Hodge was also instrumental in staging a later version of the Top Town competition in the 1980's. This was an annual variety show competition where each town put on an hour-long show with a dedicated theme at the Central Theatre,

Jean Russell (left) and David O'Brien (accompanied by wife Sarah) at the OSKA awards ceremony at Leeds Castle (June 2000). The Marlowe Shield for Best Actor stands on the table.

Chatham. The judges were local and included Paul Harris who is still very active both on stage and radio. The winning town would then compete against other Kent areas. The Gillingham entry (in which RATS members were heavily involved) won 'Best Theme' in both 1984 and 1985. Sadly, this competition was later discontinued due to lack of funds.

The Chris Crowley Award

An award much closer to home came from Chris Crowley, who was a founder member of the Oasthouse. She wished to leave her mark when she left in 1973 and presented a silver goblet to the theatre. This was to be presented on an annual basis to the person deemed to have made the greatest contribution to the society over the previous year. Members made nominations and the prize was presented at the annual dance. The last winner of this trophy was Hazel O'Brien in 1990, after which the award was no longer presented, as it was felt that many members put in a lot of hours and it seemed unfair to present only one person with an award. Also, as there were only a few members left who remembered Christine, the award was considered rather 'out of date'. More recently, the goblet has been put to use as a prop on stage!

The Concert Party

The old saying goes 'Variety is the spice of life' and over the years the RaTS have provided a range of variety shows. As well as a staple diet of drama and comedy shows at the Oasthouse Theatre, the RaTS take 'the show on the road' providing entertainment in and around Kent in the form of a travelling concert party. This provides additional income to help with the upkeep of the theatre and also helps to keep members who are not involved with productions actively involved in the society.

Doreen Cottam and Bill Beck founded the Concert Party back in 1977. The group performed under the name of 'RoAsTerS' and gave their first performance at the Oasthouse in December 1977. The name was devised as a clever amalgamation of RaTS and Oast to give a snappy title for the company.

The first concert the group performed outside the theatre was at the General Electric Company (GEC) near Rochester Airport. The group also performed concerts at the newly opened Marlborough House in Rainham as well as in Milton Regis, Linton Hospital in Coxheath and the opening of the Queen Mother Court in Borstal.

In the early days, the group would just ask for a donation to the societies funds for performing. This was usually just a token sum and they were delighted to receive £40 after one concert at Upbury Manor School in Gillingham. Whilst RaTS' most enduring musical maestro, Bill Beck, provided the music for many concerts, there were sometimes up to 6 musicians performing.

The shows included a selection of sketches, monologues and popular music and, during one particular gig at Milton Regis, an elderly lady cried throughout the concert! Enquiries afterwards reassured the entertainers that the cause was not the quality of the singing but the choice of music, which brought back so many memories.

The group had up to 17 members taking part in the concerts including one member who played the violin with his bare feet! Who said the good old days of variety were over!

When Doreen moved away from the area in the mid 1980's, the concert party folded. However, the society still provided revue style entertainment at the theatre in addition to our standard productions. In December 1987, the group performed a revue entitled 'The Oast Entertains' with members of the Folk Club, who were resident at the Oasthouse for many years, taking part.

In May 1991, the group produced *A Variety of RATS* in aid of the Medway Hospital Scanner Appeal in a concert which also featured members of the Gillingham Operatic & Dramatic Society and Medway Magical Society – another group who have used the Oasthouse Theatre as a home. In May 1996, audiences were treated to music from around the world taking in Europe, USA and the British Isles with a show entitled *RATS Around The World*.

The Concert Party 1970's style.

In the spring of 1998, RATS were approached by GEC to provide some musical entertainment for their retired members of staff. Dean Caston, with the help of Bill Beck, gathered a few members together and they gave an hours entertainment on 16 June 1998 at the venue where the original concert party had performed back in 1978.

Members enjoyed performing the concert so much that they started to meet every Monday night and presented a concert at the theatre in October of that year. In December 1998, they provided some Christmas entertainment for the Hempstead Women's Fellowship.

During 1999, things ticked over as they performed eight concerts locally, but it was after a mailshot to the Women's Institute that the Concert Party really took off! No longer were the group just providing entertainment within the Medway Towns, but were travelling around the county as far as Herne Bay, Dover and Romney Marsh. During the period April 2000 to December 2003, the group performed an impressive 42 concerts.

The group not only perform for the WI but have also entertained at 80th & 90th birthday parties, Horticultural Societies, Medway Pacemakers Club and a selection of residential homes. On a number of occasions, the group has been asked to return to venues, which is always an encouraging sign! The group has now returned to GEC Retirement Club (now BAE Systems) five times and Marlborough House in Rainham three times.

Dean Caston and Peter Gray make front page news.

Concert party organiser, Dean Caston, is a keen royalist so it is no surprise that special concerts have been performed to commemorate major royal events. In October 2000, the group performed a concert at the Oasthouse entitled *A Century Celebrates* to commemorate the 100th birthday of Her Majesty Queen Elizabeth the Queen Mother.

The concert featured words and music from across the century and the finale featured a 'Full Monty' routine performed by Dean Caston, Peter Gray and Terry Pilcher. Whilst the group did not bare quite all, one wonders what the Queen Mum would have made of it! The routine was re-created at a special charity concert in November 2001 in aid of Demelza House and was met by cheers of delight from the audience! After the show, the trio, clad only in skimpy thongs, had their photo

Our current Concert Party.

taken with Mayoress of Medway, Val Goulden. The picture made the front page of the Medway Standard with the heading of "cheeky greeting for the Mayoress". After much consideration, this routine has not been included in the running order for concerts at residential homes for the elderly, as the excitement might be too much for some of the female residents!

Special concerts have also been devised to celebrate the Queen's Golden Jubilee in 2002 and the 50th anniversary of her coronation in 2003. Both of these concerts were performed at St Margaret's Church, highlighting the important role the theatre and the church both play within the local community.

The group has grown in size since 1998 and has seen members come and go, but a dedicated band of members have stayed with the group and enjoy the thrill of performing at different venues. The spread of home made cakes and trifles, which are often provided after a concert for the WI, may also be a reason why members stay so loyal to the group! After a concert in Brenzett, the group was treated to a two course sit-down meal! However, the group does not become complacent as, at some venues, they are lucky to get a glass of water!

As well as providing involvement for members and funds for the Society, the Concert Party plays an important role in promoting the Oasthouse Theatre to a wider audience. This publicity is very welcome, as we often encounter new visitors who say "I've lived in Rainham for 20 (or 30 or 40) years and didn't know there was a theatre here". The success of the group can in some way be attributed to the GEC Retirement Club for, if they had not contacted us in 1998, the group may never have re-convened and we would not have had the opportunity to promote our theatre within the Medway Towns and far beyond. As the saying goes 'have music will travel!'

1960's Youth members take part in *Aladdin*.

1970's Junior RATS – can you spot two of the authors of this book?

The Younger Generation

The old theatrical saying 'never work with children or animals' has never been observed at the RATS, as the younger generation have played an important role in the history of the society. Youth members were enthusiastic helpers in the work to convert the building in 1963 and, forty years on, the Youth Group is still going strong.

The 'Junior RATS' (as they were known in the early days) came into being before the society acquired the Oasthouse and performed shows in St Margaret's Hall. Their first full-scale production was *Love in a Mist* in 1962, which replaced the Society's normal spring production. Youngsters not only took part in the production; they constructed and painted the scenery, provided their own props and stage-managed the show. The play was produced by Terry Ray - the only senior member involved – and it certainly seems to have been a success as the local newspaper reported, "It was a joy to see these youngsters put all they knew into the slick comedy".

In those early years, Terry Ray ran the group with the assistance of Betty Butcher and, since then, many senior members have help taken on the task with enthusiasm. Chas Hobson was in charge from the early 1970's until 1979 and, in latter years, was assisted by Melody Harbour. Other members who have nurtured the talents of our younger members include Gordon & Gill Harley, Glenda Ellis and Pam Balderston.

At first, children as young as 8 could join the group with a maximum age of 18, as this allowed a 2-year overlap with the joining age for the senior group but, during the 1970's, it was decided to raise the minimum age to 11. However, in 2001, the society hosted a series of drama workshops on Saturday mornings for 8-11 year olds. These were run by a professional tutor and proved highly successful in providing the participants with some basic drama skills and boosting their confidence.

During the 1970's and 80's, the group performed a variety of musical revues and one act plays and the talents of the group were recognised each year when the Society presented awards for acting to members of the Senior and Junior sections. Dean Caston recalls receiving a commendation for his acting in *All Things Bright and Beautiful* in 1978, when the group performed an act from the play and fellow actor and school colleague, David Watson, won the prize for Best Actor. In the early 1990's, the group split into two with a junior section and a youth group for 14-18 year olds run at different times by Frank Waslin and Tony Toms.

During 1993, the groups merged again and Ian Balderston took over the reins. Under Ian's experienced eye, they soared to new heights - winning several awards in the Duncan Rand One Act Play Festival, held each year at the Medway Little Theatre. Since most of the group were in their teens, it was decided to change the

Jeni Boyns and Andrew Balderston (centre pairing) lead the 1990's Youth production of *Ask Any Girl*.

name from Junior RATS to RATY (Rainham Amateur Theatrical Youth). It was under Ian's direction that the group started to take on the challenge of performing musicals, including excellent productions of *A Slice of Saturday Night* in 1999 and *Return to the Forbidden Planet* in 2000.

Ian's last production with the Youth group was *Annie* in November 2001, which he not only directed but also took on the role of Mr Warbucks.

With Ian taking a well-earned rest, the executive committee of the society was keen to maintain an active Youth Group and in, 2002, the RaTS decided to engage the services of a professional company - The Changeling Theatre – who have been running the group ever since. The group runs on a 10-week term and members enjoy learning the art of acting and improvisation in a fun and stimulating environment under the imaginative direction of Toby Davies.

Sadly, due to education commitments or pursuing other interests, few members of the Youth Group progress into our senior section, although some (such as Jeni Boyns and Tania Black) have returned after completing their higher education to take on major roles. Notable graduations from the Youth Section have included current Chairman Dean Caston and his wife Helen, who both started their long association with the RaTS in our Junior section and have stayed with the society ever since. Between them they have now served over 50 years!

When the group first started, members included brothers Paul & Mark Doust. Paul went on to study at the Royal Academy of Dramatic Arts (RADA) and became a professional actor and writer. He has now written several plays, which have been published by Samuel French Limited.

In September 2000, Andrew Balderston began a three-year course in acting at the Guildford School of Acting and, when he eventually hits the big time, we hope he will remember where he started his acting career!

Each year, some of the Youth Group take part in pantomime as members of the chorus and assorted minor characters, and no doubt the gruelling three or four week panto schedule (including 3 shows on a Saturday – at 2pm, 5pm and 8pm) gives them a 'kill or cure' taste of treading the boards. Over the years, our youngsters have helped to solve several casting problems in senior productions, such as Andrew Balderston and Tania Black playing the important schoolchildren characters in *The Happiest Days of Your Life* in May 1993. More recently, in recognition of the high quality and commitment displayed by the Youth Group, senior productions have been chosen with good parts for teenagers. In our January 2000 panto, *Frankenstein*, there were no fewer than seven members of the Youth group taking main parts in the story of a girls' school holiday to Transylvania. Another strong contingent from the Youth group took part in *The Darling Buds of May* in September 2000, with Liane West, Gregory Bains, Felicity Bains, Laura Beck and Simon Tomkinson playing the parts of the Larkin children, Clare Lyndon playing the Catherine Zeta Jones role of Mariette and Ila Roskilly as her love rival, Pauline Jackson.

Dean Caston recalls making his debut with the senior group when he was still a junior. "My first panto was in January 1980, but in the summer of 1980 the group were having difficulty casting three one-act plays. I was approached by the Committee and asked if I would like to take the part of Gerald Frinton in *A Prior Engagement*. I jumped at the chance and I was really excited about appearing on stage with some of the group's most experienced actors! The production even gave me the opportunity for my first stage kiss". Dean then went on to appear in the following production, *Pygmalion*, in September 1980 and the rest is part of the RaTS history.

Helen Caston recalls that, whilst appearing as a rabbit in *Snow White* in 1977, her portrayal was so convincing that a young member of the audience came onto the stage during the finale and began stroking her head!

The RaTS are committed to fostering and encouraging the talents of our younger members, in the firm belief that this is a mutually beneficial relationship, with the youngsters gaining in confidence and social skills and the society benefiting from their enthusiasm and commitment. Who knows, perhaps one of our current crop of youngsters will write the book to celebrate 75 years at the Oasthouse in 2038!

Behind the Scenes

Whilst the audience applauds the actors at the end of a production, only those who have been involved in amateur theatre will know how many unseen and unsung heroes contribute to a successful show and keep the theatre running on a day to day basis behind the scenes. From the lady serving you a cup of tea at the interval to the chap who painted the black line around the top of the set (look out for it next time you visit), many people bring energy, enthusiasm, imagination and, above all, hard work to the task of staging a play. There have been too many tireless workers over the years to bring you much more than a mere flavour of what goes on.

The Committee

Rainham Theatrical Society is a limited company run by an executive committee consisting of three officers and six other elected members. The officers are Chairman, Treasurer and Secretary, posts currently held by Dean Caston, Rose Waslin and Melody Harbour respectively. Like the other committee members, the officers are elected for a three-year term at the Annual General Meeting of the company.

The committee meets on a monthly basis to discuss and take decisions on the management of the theatre. When one considers that we have six main productions per year watched by approximately 3,000 paying customers (as well as a licensed theatre bar, Youth Group and workshops, several social events, costume hire and a Grade II listed building to maintain), the committee are running a thriving small business in what is effectively their spare time.

When the Oasthouse Theatre opened, Norman Booth was the Chairman, Brian Philpott the Treasurer and the Secretary was May Hopkins (soon to be replaced by Brian's wife, Daphne Philpott). Norman Booth had the energy and abrasiveness probably necessary to get the project off the ground, but subsequent Chairmen have been particularly noted for their diplomacy – a very necessary quality in the amateur theatre.

Norman was a bluff Yorkshireman who was managing director of a local engineering firm and President of the Gillingham Liberal Association. He had formerly been a semi-professional comedian (Charlie Norman) touring the northern club circuit. His act apparently included impressions of a parson, a schoolmaster and a fish & chip shop owner. Norman arrived in Medway in 1955 and soon joined the Rainham Amateur Theatrical Society. In 1959, he persuaded the Society to attempt pantomime for the first time, in addition to their traditional two straight plays each year. By the time the Oasthouse opened, Norman was Chairman and was heavily involved in most shows – the 1965 panto, *Aladdin*, was adapted and produced by Norman, who also played the wicked uncle, Abanazer.

In 1966, the local paper carried the story "RATS President quits after row". A couple of months earlier, Norman had been replaced as Chairman and the paper

First Oasthouse Theatre chairman, Norman Booth.

Long-serving chairmen Bill Banham (left) and Keith Sheepwash cut the cake to celebrate another anniversary. Observers include NODA rep Olga Laramman and Concert Party founder, Doreen Higgins.

reported that he intended to sever all links with the society and form his own group. His stated reason was that he felt that the RATS were doing too many shows and thus sacrificing quality. A few members recall that his departure had more to do with goings-on behind the scenes, but all acknowledge the important part Norman played in the formative years of the Oasthouse.

Norman was succeeded in 1966 by Maitland Botten and then by Brian Philpott. The next Chairman was BBC man, Bill Banham, who worked tirelessly behind the scenes during his time in office, alongside his wife Ruth, who was Secretary of the Society. During the 1970's, he worked backstage for many productions and also obtained a lot of electrical equipment for the theatre. Bill instigated many of the fund raising events around the theatre and even dressed up as Father Christmas in a specially constructed grotto in the Oasthouse. During the 1980's Ruth and Bill retired to Diss, in Norfolk, and have recently celebrated their 62nd wedding anniversary.

Keith Sheepwash joined the theatre in 1965 after seeing an advert in the local paper asking for members to help backstage. Keith went along to the group a little apprehensively, but become actively involved and was soon to take over lighting from Maitland Botten. After a spell as Treasurer, he became Chairman in 1979 and holds the record for being the RaTS longest serving Chairman. During his time, Keith guided the group through some difficult situations but with his diplomacy and calming influence he always managed to steer the members safely through the storm into smoother waters. Whilst Keith's talents are mainly behind the scenes, he has taken part in a couple of 'potted pantos' and made his main stage debut in May 1996 in the revue *Rats around the World*. When Keith stepped down in 1997 to make way for current Chairman, Dean Caston, he had been Chairman for 18 years and, rather than lose his much valued wisdom and experience, the society reinstated the role of President for Keith, who is still a respected contributor to committee discussions.

Dean Caston, became the youngest person to hold the position of Chairman and is also the first incumbent since the 1960's to regularly appear on stage. These two attributes have allowed Dean to bring a fresh perspective to the Society and his energy and commitment (strongly supported by his wife, Helen, whom he met at the Oasthouse) have resulted in many fresh ideas as the Society entered the new millennium. Dean oversaw the refurbishment of the seats in the auditorium, launched the 'Spend a Penny' appeal to raise money for a cast/disabled toilet and pushed through the refurbishment of the Green Room. In our 40th anniversary year, Dean is ably assisted in his duties by the watchful and diligent book keeping of Treasurer, Rose Waslin, and by our longest-serving officer, Secretary, Melody Harbour.

Since 2001, the committee have supplied a 'Duty Manager' for each performance who is there to greet and assist the audience, deal with any problems that may arise and ensure that the theatre is complying with Health and Safety obligations. And, just in case you thought that being on the committee sounds glamorous, Duty Manager duties included unblocking the loos on many occasions prior to drain repairs in 2003.

Backstage Crew

We now usually have the luxury of five or six weeks to build the set for each production (as opposed to one or two nights in the pre-Oasthouse days), but the task still requires a talented stage manager and a dedicated crew. Fred Haddell was stage manager for the first Oasthouse production (Billy Liar) and he shared SM duties mainly with Jack Butcher and Len Turner during the early 1960's. Setbuilding was not solely a male domain, however, and Betty Butcher and Diane Yeman both took their turns in charge of the stage crew. Later in the 60's, Neville Crane and Dave Waters worked on many sets, before Bill Banham and his son-in-law, Tony Ellis, took over the reins in the 1970's.

Setbuilding at the Oasthouse presents a unique range of problems due to the size of the stage, access only being possible from one side (the other is the outside wall of the building) and several awkwardly placed oak beams which hold together our listed building. The mid 1970's saw the arrival of a Stage Manager who was up to the challenge of all these obstacles – Steve Harbour. Steve worked creatively with many directors to design and construct some of the greatest sets seen at the Oasthouse, including Anne Frank's house in 1993 complete with upstairs room. Steve has worked backstage on more RATS productions than anyone else and now holds the position of Resident Stage Manager, offering support and advice to anyone else who takes up the stage management challenge.

In November 1983, an all-female backstage crew received extensive coverage in the local press for constructing the set and working backstage for the Francis

Durbridge thriller, *Suddenly at Home*. Pauline Harley, Doreen Higgins and Jacky Giddings spent many hours during the day building the set and their determination to keep it an all-female crew certainly kept the male members away.

During the 1990's, Ivan Jenner and Gary Wyatt formed a successful stage management partnership. They particularly enjoyed working backstage during pantomime and often mischievously set challenges for cast members (such as working the name of a fruit into their lines), whilst keeping spirits up with assorted penalties for bad behaviour and awards and certificates for contributions to the general hilarity of panto.

The actual flats used for setbuilding are constantly in need of repair, as they are moved around so much (and so clumsily) during the year. We generally need to replace them about once every ten years and it is difficult to get sufficiently skilled people to build them (at a price we can afford). Len Turner built our original set of flats in the 1960's and these were replaced in 1977 when the father of long-time member, Steve Hewlett, offered to build a set of flats together with a new cyclorama. Around this time, new backdrops (for pantomime) were built by Bill Banham and these were stored in the space underneath the auditorium, until it was discovered that this area had developed damp. Our current set of flats was built in 1991 and the kiln where they are stored was fitted with racking to store them safely.

Setbuilding can be a dangerous occupation. In 1980, Bill Garlick was working on the pantomime set during the day when he fell from a stepladder and broke his ankle. In the days before mobile phones, Bill faced an uncomfortable crawl downstairs to raise the alarm on the public phone on the foyer. A rule was subsequently introduced that no member may work alone in the theatre.

This may be just as well, since the theatre is reputed to be haunted. The Oasthouse ghost dates back to 1897 when a gentleman named Mortimer Squires discovered the liaison his young and beautiful wife was having with a thresher who worked in the Oasthouse. As the young lovers eloped, Squires followed them on horseback and caught up with them in Upchurch, where he killed them both. Frightened at his deed, he returned and hid in the Oasthouse, where his body was later discovered in one of the drying rooms – dangling from the end of a rope. Despite his real name, the ghost is now known as 'Fred' and several members are convinced they have felt a ghostly presence or heard inexplicable noises in the theatre.

To date, only one person has spent a full night alone at the Oasthouse Theatre, although this was a mishap rather than an act of bravado. In September 1988, Jeffrey Marsh was cleaning the stage after the dress rehearsal for *Counter Crime* when the last member left from downstairs and locked the front door. As he didn't have a set of keys and as he didn't want to disturb anyone at that time of night, Jeffrey settled down for a nap in one of the armchairs on the set. When dawn broke, he phoned the police and was finally rescued by Rosina Fletcher.

Lighting

The first Oasthouse productions were lit by footlights, but these were replaced with overhead lights after the footlights got wet and exploded during one of our

Another successful costume drama – *My Cousin Rachel* in 1999.

early pantomimes. These pantomimes also featured follow spotlights at the back of the auditorium in the spaces now occupied by seats G1 and G12 (the end seats of the back row). Lighting and electrics was exclusively the preserve of Maitland Botten from the opening of the Oasthouse until 1966, when he was joined by a young Keith Sheepwash.

Over the decades, our lighting equipment has developed from the primitive to the sophisticated system we have today, from a cramped corner backstage to a fully enclosed lighting box with an excellent view of the stage (and the audience – yes, we can see if you are nodding off!). Many RATS members have controlled the lights over the years, perhaps most notably Steve Hewlett, Neil Balderston and his brother Ian Balderston, who is our current electrics manager.

Wardrobe

There have been many great wardrobe mistresses at the Oasthouse, beginning with Zena Haddell, who had the advantage of being a tailoress by profession. In later years, the needle was taken up by the likes of Phyll Hobson, Joy Garlick, Melody Harbour and Janine Hewlett. The role was performed intermittently, and with impressive knowledge and attention to detail, by Rosina Fletcher. When Rosina emigrated to Cyprus with her husband Clive in 2001, Beryl Lacey took over as wardrobe mistress and has overseen a comprehensive makeover for the wardrobe kiln. This kiln has housed the costumes since 1984, when they were moved from the area behind the bar. As many dated back to the opening of the theatre and were becoming scarce and even valuable, it was decided to allocate a secure environment for their storage.

We often hire costumes out to other societies, local schools and individuals looking for fancy dress. Thanks to our extensive collection and the talents of our wardrobe workers, we rarely have to hire costumes for our own shows and have

52

been able to stage lavishly costumed shows such as *Camelot, My Cousin Rachel, When We are Married, Frankenstein the Panto* and, in our 40th anniversary year, *Lord Arthur Savile's Crime*.

Properties

Our props collection shares kiln space with our wardrobe. Directors and actors often spend hours scouring charity and second hand shops searching out the right prop for a particular play. Some members, such as Kathy West, have the creative abilities to build magnificent props from scratch.

Our most celebrated props master of the last 40 years has been Bob Higgins. Bob was a genius in obtaining awkward props and charming his way to 'freebies' for a play. For our 1984 pantomime, *Aladdin*, Bob borrowed a lamp from the London Palladium, which had been used in their own production. For *Deathtrap* in March 1986, he obtained free supplies of Budweiser beer (relatively unknown in the 1980's) and Canada Dry Ginger ale. For the same play, Bob created a garrotte made from a length of tubing with fine holes which allowed 'blood' to flow out at the appropriate moment.

Our current props master is Jack Homewood, who has built up an encyclopaedic knowledge of the items we have acquired over the years and jealously guards our collection.

Other duties

The many other tasks necessary to the smooth running of the theatre include running the licensed bar (rehearsals and performances) and the tea bar (performance nights); selling programmes and raffle tickets (and sweets during pantomime season); taking telephone and postal bookings for plays; manning the box office on production nights; producing posters, newsletters and programmes; delivering posters and leaflets to local shops and libraries; taking photographs of productions (usually at dress rehearsal); writing publicity material and contacting local press and media; maintaining the fabric of the building; reading plays to select the programme for each year; collecting membership fees and issuing membership cards (and payment reminders); organising fundraising activities such as our lottery bonus ball competition; and other one off activities such as obtaining quotes for building work and meeting contractors at the Theatre.

With all this activity taking place, it is amazing that we find people willing to give so much of their time, but we usually do. Occasionally there are problems; in 1987 it was so difficult to find volunteers to man the bar that the committee sent out a compulsory bar rota telling members when they had to run the bar. This was not well received, especially as members were also informed that they would not be considered for acting roles if they were deemed to be 'not pulling their weight'. Happily, incidents such as this are few and far between and many members put in countless hours of unpaid work for the society.

So next time you find yourself applauding the cast at the end of another enjoyable performance, dedicate a bit of that applause to the people who made it all possible by working behind the scenes.

Memorable productions

All of our productions have been memorable to someone for one reason or another. The reason may be that the play was well performed and well received; possibly there was a humorous or unusual incident during rehearsals or, more memorable still, during a performance; or it may be for a purely personal reason, such as one's first time on stage – an experience etched on most people's memory for ever.

For many actors (and audience as well) the annual Oasthouse pantomime has provided a memorable first experience of live theatre. Our 2002 panto, *Frankenstein–The Panto*, ran for 18 performances over 3 weeks on alternate Thursday nights, each Friday Night and three performances on Saturdays – at 2pm, 5pm and 8pm. Given that the running time was 2 hours 20 minutes, performers had little more than half an hour between shows to rest and grab a bite to eat. Previous pantos have run for 20 or more performances, including four on one Saturday and the occasional Sunday matinee.

In this chapter we will look at some other interesting shows from the Oasthouse archives. The choice of productions which follows is, of course, subjective, but hopefully they give a flavour of some significant, interesting or amusing occasions over our 40 years at the Oasthouse Theatre.

Billy Liar November 1963 & November 1981

The first production staged at the Oasthouse Theatre was revived to celebrate our 18th birthday in 1981. The original cast included many key figures in the birth of the theatre, such as Betty Butcher, Peter Yeman, Zena Haddell, Christine Crowley and Brenda Pearson, who played Billy's grandmother and who thus claims the distinction of being the first person to appear on the Oasthouse stage. The play was produced by Norman Booth, who was theatre chairman at its opening, and stage manager was Fred Haddell, who had played such a key role in converting the building. The title role was taken by Terry Ray who, according to the first newspaper review of an Oasthouse production, played the role "remarkably well, adjusting his moods cleverly while sustaining the main characterisation". Praise also went to the stage crew who had built a set "cleverly designed to fit the small stage" and to producer, Norman Booth, who had "clearly used his available material to the best advantage". For the dress rehearsal, Les Hopkins (who played Billy's father) was unavailable, so Norman Booth read in the part and consequently appears in the only surviving photos of the production.

When the play was revived in 1981, Brenda Pearson was the only member of the original cast still playing an active role in the society and she achieved the remarkable feat of playing Billy's mother 18 years after playing his gran! The title role this time was taken by Bill Beck and the cast also featured Brian Erratt, Janet May and David O'Brien.

The Late Edwina Black 1964

The programme for this production identifies the producer as 'The Late Charles Moss' because, sadly, he died a few weeks before the opening night. Stage manager, Jack Butcher, stepped in to take over direction and the production went ahead starring Peter Yeman, Brenda Pearson, Norman Booth and Betty Butcher. This production also featured the grand opening of the theatre bar, which had been delayed due to difficulties in obtaining a licence. Some members of the audience may have been glad of a stiff drink after one particular performance as, towards the end of the third act, a mouse invaded the auditorium and ran up the side gangway. The local newspaper noted that "the perambulations of the adventurous mouse rather distracted some of the audience" from the denouement of this thriller.

Aladdin January 1965

Aladdin's lamp wasn't quite so magical during one performance of our second pantomime at the Oasthouse, when all of the lights in the building fused at the start of the second half. Illuminated only by a solitary gas lamp and the Chinese lantern props used in the show, the audience showed true RATS spirit by working its way through a series of well-known community songs, while an electrician worked feverishly to mend the blown fuse. They had to sing unaccompanied, as Jim Layzell's Hammond electric organ was also temporarily out of action during the incident. On resumption of the action, impromptu jokes were added to the script and the local paper was happy to hail another success.

Starring in her debut production was RATS Secretary, Daphne Philpott. The story goes that she was watching auditions and was persuaded to have a bash, landing the plum role of Princess So-Shi at her first attempt. Norman Booth's portrayal of the wicked Abanazer was so convincing that one little girl had to be removed screaming from the audience. The local paper commented that the incident "will no doubt give her a serious neurosis against painted, paunchy magicians for life". One can only hope that this did not have too serious an effect on her adult years.

Merry Switzerland 1966 & 1972

This bright musical was written by two former pupils of Gillingham Grammar School, Bernard Mitchell (who worked in Barclays Bank in Rainham) and Alan Wilcox. It was based on a story by Edward Young of Hoo, near Rochester and was set in a village inn on a Swiss mountainside. A beautiful and innocent young innkeeper's daughter is lured away from her village boyfriend by a visiting American, but all ends happily with a quadruple wedding. Mitchell and Wilcox accompanied on piano and accordion respectively and Val Warn (Valerie Lawrence at the time) played Maria, the Innkeeper's daughter, with a reported "childish delight". The local reporter was moved to call it "one of the happiest, most sparkling productions I have seen for a long time".

The musical, which had first been staged at the Mountbatten Club in 1962, was revived due to popular demand in 1972. This time, Bernard Mitchell actually appeared in the show as Clive, accompanied by RATS stalwarts Chris Crowley, Val

The Oasthouse Theatre. Rainham. Kent

The RATS present their musical for 1972

MERRY SWITZERLAND

PROGRAMME 5p

The programme for *Merry Switzerland* (1972) captured the joyous spirit of the show.

The Smugglers take refuge in a cave in our 1983 production. Peter O'Brien (kneeling) and George Stockford are centre stage.

Warn (now married), David Waters and Glenda Banham, who took the part of Maria.

The Oasthouse Theatre has also staged *Holiday of a Lifetime* and *Once Upon an Island* (twice) by the same authors.

The Smuggler & The Lady / Nerina 1967, 1983 and 2003

In November 1966, Brenda Pearson wrote the story of *Nerina*, about a family who are holidaying in Cornwall when they have a car accident and have to spend the night in a cave – haunted by the ghost of Nerina. By March 1967, 17 songs had been added by Bernard Mitchell & Alan Wilcox and in October 1967, RATS audiences were able to follow the adventures of the Packer family as they travelled back 300 years to the days of Cornish smuggling. The Packer parents were played by real life husband and wife, Fred and Zena Haddell, Hilary Booth played Nerina and Brenda Pearson herself played twittery Aunt Maud. The atmospheric set even featured real running water tumbling over the rocks.

For our September 1983 production, the story of Nerina was transformed into *The Smuggler & The Lady*. This time, the music was written by Bill Beck and the lyrics were provided by Brenda Pearson and Pauline Harley. This production featured husband and wife teams in Peter & Hazel O'Brien and Bob & Doreen Higgins, as well as the excellent singing voice of Alex Bushell and the intense acting of Gary Robinson.

As part of our 40th anniversary celebrations, *The Smuggler & The Lady* was revived in September 2003, with Jeni Boyns playing *Nerina*. This makes it the only show (apart from panto) to have been performed at the Oasthouse on 3 separate occasions.

The Lion in Winter 1974 & 1983

This tale of King Henry II and his Queen Eleanor was given added resonance during its run in 1974, when power cuts meant that some performances took place by candlelight, no doubt giving a highly authentic atmosphere of 12th century life. The elegant and talented actress Grace Murrell repeated her performance as Eleanor nine years later, with Michael Harley having graduated from her son to her husband. Producer Gary Robinson and stage manager Pauline Harley achieved the 3-d effect of the stone walls in a French castle for this production by constructing them out of copies of the Gay News, giving actors a different slant on current events until they were painted in. There was a certain relevance in this choice of building material, as the play hints at a homosexual relationship between Richard the Lionheart and Philippe, King of France – a scene which drew murmurs of disapproval from the conservative RATS audiences of the 1980's

Just the Ticket 1975 & 1981

Few plays over the years have caused more laughter at the Oasthouse than this story about a traffic warden, Harry Lovelock, whose two hobbies are morris-dancing and collecting stuffed birds. Both productions had late cast alterations with Roy Evans having just a couple of weeks to rehearse the lead role in 1975 and Beryl Lacey stepping in at the last minute to play Ethel Lovelock in 1983. Director on both occasions was Peter O'Brien, who recalls that the serious morris-dancing group who were brought in to help with authenticity became most upset when they realised that everyone was laughing at them. However, the biggest laugh of the show was for a stuffed owl. This amazing prop was created by Brenda Pearson and Chris Murrell and featured flashing light bulb eyes. At one stage, Harry finds a wad of money stuffed up the bird's rear end and the line "No wonder his eyes lit up" brought the house down every night.

This Happy Breed July 1977

As part of the celebrations for Queen Elizabeth II's Silver Jubilee, RATS ran a competition, in conjunction with the Evening Post newspaper, to choose the 'Play of the Reign' to be performed at the Oasthouse Theatre. The judges included Evening Post critic Kieron Wood and RATS own Glenda Ellis. The competition was won by Ruth Banham (by coincidence Glenda's mum), who was presented with a commemorative silver plate for suggesting Noel Coward's classic piece. The play chronicles the lives of the Gibbons family over a 20 year period from 1919 to 1939, played out in the dining room of their house in Clapham. Demonstrating the passage of time is a particular challenge in this play and director Peter O'Brien and Stage Manager Steve Harbour came up with an ingenious 'set within a set'. After the inner set of flats was removed during the interval (no mean feat given the size of our stage and backstage area), the audience were presented with a change of wallpaper for the second half of the play. Peter particularly remembers the play for an excellent performance by Keri Howell, a highly talented young actor who was tragically killed in a road accident a few years later. As a sign of how things have changed in the second half of the Queen's reign, it is interesting that the local paper reported of the main character (played by Gordon Harley) "Mr Gibbons delighted several of the audience by smoking Gold Flake throughout the production".

Couples 1979

November 1979 saw the world premiere at the Oasthouse of this play by local playwright Bettine Manktelow, one year after we staged another of her plays, *They Call it Murder*. *Couples* told the stories of three couples who make use of a Brighton hotel bedroom for lovemaking. The first act was set during a political conference and Bettine (a former member of Gillingham Labour Party) claims to have drawn on her knowledge of Labour conferences to create the lecherous Scottish MP, who tries to seduce a party worker. Acts two and three featured the room as a bedsit and a squat, with progressively seedier characters using the love nest. Unusually for a RATS production, the play contained "much disrobing and swearing". Guests on opening night included Conservative local councillors, the author herself and the appropriately named John Bedding, from Samuel French, who were considering publishing the play.

Later that month, the author wrote to producer Brenda Pearson to say that she was very pleased with the show. She added that she was now working at the Folkestone Theatre, where the manager (although impressed with the script) felt that *Couples* was a little too risqué for Folkestone.

Lock up Your Daughters 1985

Two of the main constraints in producing a play at the Oasthouse are the limited size of the stage and the restricted access to it. Chris Williams had the imagination and enthusiasm to squeeze large productions onto a small stage, as he later proved with *Camelot*. Bernard Miles musical, *Lock up Your Daughters* (an adaptation of Henry Fielding's Rape Upon Rape, with lyrics by Lionel Bart), had been presented at London's Mermaid Theatre, rather than one of the capital's larger venues and so was relatively unknown to audiences and cast members alike. The show was described as colourful, bawdy, witty and boisterous, describing the corrupt practices of a magistrate, Mr Justice Squeezum. Added piquancy was given to RATS' production as Squeezum was played by Peter O'Brien, a serving Medway magistrate.

The show was packed with songs that were fun to sing and a delight to hear, such as 'I read it in the papers so it must be true' and 'When will the ravishing begin', which ended with the dashing Ramble (Alex Bushell) in bed with Mrs Squeezum (Grace Murrell). When the show ran in Boston, the local police had threatened to close down the production if the actor and actress were actually in bed together on the stage. The play ran at the Oasthouse for three weeks (rather than the usual two) and throughout the run there was a waiting list for cancelled bookings.

Steve Berry shows off his silver service skills in *Quiet Affairs*, 1994. Beryl Lacey and Mike Newvell admire his prowess.

Quiet Affairs 1994

After reaching the final of the Kent Drama Festival for the previous two years, with *The March on Russia* and *The Diary of Anne Frank*, director Chris Williams was determined to pull out all the stops for our 1994 festival entry. The play, written by Tony Onwin (who had adjudicated the festival two years earlier), was set in a restaurant. Stage manager Steve Harbour created a two level set with fully fitted carpet and Steve Berry, who played Lance the waiter, was sent to catering college for three sessions to learn the rudiments of silver service. During the performance, all six actors were served with (and ate) a hot main course (including vegetarian dish for Mike Newvell) and dessert. The meals were prepared in a microwave oven backstage and had to be served with perfect timing to ensure that no serving took place during dialogue at a particular table.

The Vigil 2000

This play by little known playwright Ladislas Fodor was our entry for the On Stage in Kent Awards in 2000. More importantly, it was a community production, involving members of other societies and parishioners of St Margaret's Church in

lack of authentic strawberry baskets!) and an extra performance was necessary in the second week to cope with demand for tickets.

Leading members of the cast also posed for publicity photos at Riverside Country Park in Gillingham, replicating the famous pose from the TV series and the Society was delighted to receive good luck messages from David Jason (Pop Larkin) and Philip Franks (Charley) which are proudly displayed in the Green Room.

In the 1980's, actors from the theatre also dressed appropriately to perform a homegrown piece entitled *Bastards and Bitches* for the Richard III Society at their mediaeval banquet in Canterbury. Although we are used to performing on a small stage, the acting area for this venue was little more than a rostrum, so most of the dialogue had to be performed without much movement. The drama was set to music by Bill Beck and Bob Nicholls, although they did this independently of each other as other commitments prevented them from meeting to share ideas.

RaTS have also performed at Medway Hospital (and later at the Oasthouse Theatre) for the junior outpatients, many of whom had serious or even terminal illness and who otherwise would not have been able to attend an Oasthouse production. These 'mini-pantomimes' and 'mini-dramas' were largely home-written and loosely based on traditional pantomime, for example *Princess Lucinda*, *Snow White and Rose Red* and a parody of Noddy titled *Little Shoddy*. The programme for *Snow White and Rose Red*, written and directed by Peter O'Brien, announced that the audience were to be privileged to see 'The world premiere performance' (history tells us that this could more accurately have been labelled 'The world's only performance'). So audience-friendly were the performers that the only sweets thrown to the audience during the show were suitable for diabetics! This was certainly a rewarding venture and it was a joy to see the smiling faces of the brave children who attended these events.

Many theatre trips have been organised by the RaTS. These are normally purely recreational and, generally speaking, not to study the work of a particular playwright or group. We have seen *The Beautiful Game*, *Dancing at Lughnasa*, *Blood Brothers*, *Don't Dress for Dinner*, to name but a few, in the West End and *Sweet Charity* and *Some Like it Hot* at Bromley's Churchill Theatre.

However, many of these outings have been plagued with transport difficulties! A group of members eagerly waited on Longfield station for the train to take them to London to see a performance of *Dancing at Lughnasa*. When they realised they were faced with engineering works and long delays, they jumped into their cars and drove to Bromley to pick up a train to London. Upon arrival at Victoria, they hailed a taxi and were then caught up in a demonstration in Trafalgar Square. They abandoned the taxi and dashed across the Square to arrive at the Garrick Theatre just before curtain up!

Heavy snow in February 1991 meant that several members who were due to attend a performance of *Time and The Conways* at the Old Vic decided to cancel the visit. However, a small band of members braved the weather and drove to London. They were rewarded with a tour of the National Theatre complex before sitting back to watch a matinee performance of the play and then battling through the snow on their return to Rainham.

In March 2001, 13 members travelled to London to see Ben Elton & Andrew Lloyd Webber's *The Beautiful Game*, with 2 members coming straight to the West End from a matinee performance of another play at the Churchill Theatre. Tube strikes made the journey home somewhat difficult! After the show members found Oxford Circus tube station closed and the queues at bus stops longer than the rush hour! Work commitments meant that Dean Caston was driving up to Birmingham after the show and he arrived at his destination before the rest of the party arrived back in Medway!

Members experienced less stress when they travelled to Diss, Norfolk in September 1996 to see former member, Graham Sessions, appear in a production performed by the Mere Players.

David O'Brien was a member of the National Youth Theatre from 1981 to 1983 and a trip was organised to see him in *For Those in Peril*, a play about the 1931 Invergordon naval mutiny, at London's Shaw Theatre in 1983. Whilst at the NYT, David appeared in productions with Liza Tarbuck, Gina McKee and Nathaniel Parker and later achieved his own fifteen minutes of fame as an extra in the BBC TV series *The Monocled Mutineer*, written by Alan Bleasdale and starring Paul McGann, Timothy West and Penelope Wilton (eagle-eyed RATS members spotted David holding Timothy West at gunpoint).

Members also made several trips to the National Portrait Gallery in London to see former member Kathy Beck perform with Marchurst productions.

There have been various trips to local theatres by members who have followed festival adjudicators to rival productions – both to weigh up the opposition and to get an insight into the character, likes and dislikes of the adjudicator before he (or she) visits the Oasthouse! During 1992, many of those involved with *The March on Russia* (led by director, Chris Williams) spent many evenings, some enjoyable, some not – watching rival groups perform their festival entries.

Lamberhurst Vineyards and a visit to the Owl House Gardens was the venue for a summer outing in 1990 and this proved to be another eventful day out! Whilst strolling round the grounds of Owl House, Melody Harbour decided to test the temperature of the swimming pool and bent over to feel the water. A splash in the water alerted her to the fact that she had inadvertently dropped her car keys into the deep water. No-one else present looked fit enough to be able to recover the keys so, whilst all the men present were made to avert their eyes, Melody stripped naked and dived in to retrieve them. Unable to reach them, she borrowed a magnet and eventually located the missing keys. Some people just don't know when to stop performing! Needless to say this outing made the headlines in the local paper. One wag commented that Melody had a barefaced cheek to go to such extremes to get publicity for the theatre!

The theatre bar is a focal point within the building – many a happy hour is spent there during rehearsal nights and after performances – and, as purveyors of Shepherd Neame's fine ales, we have been invited to visit their brewery on a regular basis over the past few years. The first part of the tour showcases the entire beer-making process, which in itself is very interesting, but the best part comes at the end of the tour, when guests are invited to sample, free of charge, the various products of the brewery. One's glass may be re-filled with the liquid of one's choice, as long as it has been emptied of the previous brew. Unsurprisingly, this is one of our most popular trips; some members have been so often that they could almost act as the guide. The post-tour activity is always well worth another visit.

Often, the tour is followed by a pub crawl round Faversham and many members have been left wondering how they found their way back to Rainham! Peter Gray, a local church stalwart, respected civil servant and former RaTS Treasurer has asked us not to mention the time that he fell asleep in a Canterbury nightclub after a particularly thorough inspection of the brewery.

On a more serious note, as members of the Little Theatre Guild of Great Britain, RaTS delegates have attended various functions and meetings since joining the Guild in 1995. They have travelled across the United Kingdom to Leeds, Birmingham, Newport and Southport and nearer to home to Whitstable and Tonbridge.

These conferences provide an excellent opportunity to network with fellow members, admire the facilities and examine the ways in which different theatres operate.

Most conferences are held over the weekend and normally follow the same format. Upon arrival at the host theatre on a Saturday morning, visitors are treated to a guided tour of the building. After a welcome speech, there are normally a selection of workshops to choose from covering speech, movement, improvisation, marketing, youth theatre and a variety of technical workshops covering scenery, lighting and stage management.

In the evening, members attend a performance given by the host group followed by supper and a chance to mingle with fellow LTG members. It is often reassuring to talk to other groups and find that their theatres also suffer with problems of casting productions or finding willing members to take on some of the responsibility for running a theatre. Workshops continue on Sunday and after lunch members wend their way back home brimming with enthusiasm and new ideas for their theatre.

In April 1996 travelling problems meant that members attending the 50th anniversary conference in Leeds were somewhat delayed. Helen and Dean Caston, accompanied by Frank Waslin, Treasurer at that time, set off from Kent at 3.00pm. They were met with delays on the M25 and then hit with a freak snowstorm, which caused the car to break down. The three tired travellers finally arrived in Leeds at midnight! After a good night's sleep, they were ready to face the day ahead and put on their best bib and tucker for the gala anniversary dinner held at Leeds University. Fortunately, the journey home was less eventful.

Whilst it is always interesting to visit other theatres and attend social events, members are always pleased to come back to our charming theatre and it does make us appreciate how fortunate we are to have the excellent facilities of our converted Oasthouse. As the saying goes...'There's no place like home' and, considering the hours some members spend at the theatre, the Oasthouse truly is a second home to many of us!

Visitors & Guests

In 40 years, the RaTS have played host to a variety of special guests and professional entertainers who have helped to raise the profile of the Oasthouse. However, before we look at some of these individuals and the impact they have made on the theatre, we should not forget our most important visitors - our audience! We are fortunate to have a dedicated band of supporters, many of whom have been attending productions for decades. Our loyal audiences are generous with their praise and are always willing to forgive the occasional lapse in our high standards, safe in the knowledge that commitment, enthusiasm and a warm welcome are never lacking at the Oasthouse. However, we know that it is never safe to rest on our laurels and are always looking for opportunities to attract new audiences and raise awareness of our theatre.

The RATS were grateful to have Dickie Henderson as Patron of the theatre for many years. Whilst he did not visit the theatre, he kept in touch with theatre news up until his death in September 1985.

In March 1986, Roy Hudd took over as our Patron. This followed an introduction from musical maestro and RATS member, Bob Nicholls, who played the piano for Roy when he started out in showbusiness nearly 50 years ago. Roy, of course, has now established himself as one of the country's most creative and talented entertainers with his own regular "News Huddlines" radio show and many West End appearances including Fagin in *Oliver*. In 1982, he won 'Best Actor in a Musical' for his portrayal of Bud Flanagan in the hit musical *Underneath the Arches*. RATS Chairman, Dean Caston, met Roy Hudd with Bob shortly after he became patron and recalls *"Roy was a charming gentleman and made us so welcome when we visited him in his dressing room at Bromley's Churchill Theatre. He was particularly interested in the history of our theatre"*. Roy visited the Oasthouse and had lunch during the mid 1990's after paying a visit to the Theatre Royal project in Chatham.

It is always a pleasure to welcome the author of the play being performed to witness a production, although there is always the fear that we may not have interpreted the piece in quite the way the author intended.

In November 1979, the RATS staged the world premiere of *Couples* by Bettine Manktelow, who attended one of the performances (see Memorable productions). In January 1991, Leonard Caddy came to see a performance of his pantomime *Cinderella* and he can't have been too unhappy as he allowed us to stage another of his pantos, *Jack and the Beanstalk*, two years later.

Local entertainer, Bobby Bragg (whose father Billy owned the bicycle shop in Livingstone Circus, Gillingham) made several appearances at the theatre during the early 1970's in a variety club set up by Jimmy Hodge called 'Ace of Clubs'. The club was established in 1974 and used the theatre to rehearse in and perform shows. Bobby went on to appear in the West End and is a currently one of the top warm-up men for TV shows.

In March 1980, Joy & Bill Garlick started a weekly Folk Club at the Oasthouse and welcomed many special guests from that music scene to the Oasthouse, such as folk legends, The Yetties, in 1981.

In March 1980, Liverpool poet, Roger McGough, performed at the Oasthouse as part of the Gillingham Arts Festival, but when we contacted him to see if he had any memories of his visit to the theatre, he emailed the poetic reply: *'Sorry Mr. Caston, my memory ain't that good. Best wishes, Roger Mcg'*. A year later, in March 1981, another of the Liverpool poets, Brian Patten, gave a reading at the theatre.

The Medway Magical Society used to meet in the Club Room each month and have performed a selection of shows over the years including *Nothing Up My Sleeve* in November 1980 and *A Magical Evening* in November 1991.

Special guests from the radio have also played an important part in the RaTS history. In November 1970, the long running BBC radio programme *Down Your Way* came to the theatre to record a programme. Brian Philpott and secretary, Ruth Banham, were interviewed by Franklin Engleman. A piece of music was also chosen, Rachmaninoff's 2nd piano Concerto, which was being used in the play *Five Finger Exercise*.

On 1st October 1999 Barbara Sturgeon from BBC Radio Kent broadcast the whole of her show 'live' from the Oasthouse Theatre. She interviewed RATS members and interspersed with the discussions were monologues performed by Brenda Pearson and songs from Nora Huff. A local resident listening to the broadcast later turned up at the theatre, as he had worked in the Oast prior to its conversion. Our special guest for the broadcast was Peter Denyer, who had appeared in the TV comedy series, *Please Sir*. Peter is the author of many pantomimes, including *Mother Goose* which was performed at the theatre the following January.

Paul Harris, also from BBC Radio Kent, is another great supporter of the Oasthouse. He often reviews our productions on his weekly radio programme and has himself appeared on stage at the theatre. In March 1999, he wrote and appeared in *Titter Not* about the life of comedian, Frankie Howerd. Paul has appeared in over 30 pantomimes and has written one of the most authoritative books on the subject. Paul writes the following about the RaTS:

"For many years I have been a visitor to the Oasthouse Theatre attending on average two or three productions a year and am always delighted at the welcome I receive.

"I have always said that an evening at a theatre starts from the moment you enter the doors. A good play, well acted, can be spoilt by surly staff or a too cold or too hot theatre. At the Oasthouse Theatre you experience the feel good factor as soon as you enter the building. You are always welcomed with a smile from the front of house staff. The tiny upstairs theatre has a friendly feel about it and has managed to capture that magical atmosphere that can all too often be found lacking in many, far larger, modern theatres.

RaTS chairman Dean Caston meets Radio Kent presenter Barbara Sturgeon and playwright Peter Denyer.

"It is highly probable that without amateur theatre there would be no professional theatre. Many of our top actors started off in local amateur companies, as did many designers, stage managers, electricians and musicians. The RaTS have held workshops as well as running junior and senior sections for both on stage and back stage positions. It is therefore not just a hobby for children and adults but an important training ground for all sorts of people. RaTS realised this many years ago and this is what makes them so successful.

"Another thing that always strikes me whenever I visit the Oasthouse Theatre is how smoothly it all seems to run and how high the standard of productions generally is.

"I've no doubt that, like most companies, they've had their disasters and arguments over the years, but it's never allowed to show and, knowing something about the work and worry that goes into producing a show and running a theatre, it never ceases to amaze me just how polished it all seems to be whenever I visit.

"When you realise that not only have RaTS produced plays, musicals and pantomimes, for the past forty years, as well as training thousands of young actors and playing host to dozens of visiting companies, but they also built the theatre themselves, just saying congratulations doesn't seem enough, but what else can I say...I'm gob-smacked."

In September 2002 Paul returned to the theatre with fellow broadcaster, Paul James, to perform a stage version of their hit radio show The Saturday Carry On.

Local radio stars Paul Harris and Paul James are strong supporters of the Oasthouse Theatre.

Friend of the Oasthouse, Marie Sumner, appearing as A Lady of the Naughty Nineties.

Professional entertainer Mrs Marie Sumner, "The Lady of the Naughty Nineties" (the 1890's) has also been a keen supporter of the theatre since first appearing at the Oasthouse in 1995. Marie performs her one woman Victorian soirée to packed houses around the county and has also appeared at the Leeds City Varieties, where the hit BBC show *The Good Old Days* was recorded for over 30 years. In September 2001 and March 2003, Marie performed at the Oasthouse in aid of the building fund. She also performed her rousing 'Last Night of the Proms' finale at concerts to celebrate the Queen's Golden Jubilee and 50th anniversary of the coronation. Marie had these kind words about the Oasthouse:

"It was when I was appearing as a guest in a professional show, that I first discovered the Oasthouse Theatre and was immediately enchanted! I thought it was amazing that an actual Oasthouse, part of our heritage here in Kent, had been so lovingly and skilfully converted. Since that time, I have been delighted to hire the building for my own One-Woman Shows, and it has been during that time that I have found there is so much more to the Oasthouse. It is maintained and run to the utmost efficiency - in fact - to the level of any professional establishment, but best of all are the company of people who operate there.

"They are all dedicated in producing entertainment of the highest standard. Everyone is encouraged to develop their own skills, whether it is actually treading

the boards or in a technical capacity, such as set building, lighting or wardrobe. It's a real joy to see how they all work to bring entertainment to the locals, who would otherwise have to travel much further afield. A nicer group of people would be hard to find and every newcomer is warmly welcomed. How lucky Rainham is to have had those far-thinking people, who originally had the courage and inspiration, all those years ago, to start such an imaginative and successful project. It's one of Kent's hidden Gems!"

Over the years we have played host to a number of professional companies including Dual Control, who performed a show entitled *Grimaldi* about the famous clown in May 1987, and the Channel Theatre Company, who staged *The Lesson* by Eugene Ionesco a few years earlier. The Changeling Theatre Company have been regular visitors during the past few years. They have performed at the theatre in conjunction with Medway Arts Festival, with original shows such as *Five Go to Fishy Bottom* and *The World is Just About Enuff*.

Marchurst Productions performed several of their works at the theatre during the mid 1990's. Kathy Clancy, a former member of the RaTS, joined forces with Colin Pinney after appearing in our festival production *The March On Russia* in March 1992 (Colin was the adjudicator). Kathy initiated and researched many of their productions including *My Unhappy Brother* the story of Branwell Bronte and his sisters and *The Path to Milkwood*, The Dylan Thomas Story. They performed several times at the National Portrait Gallery in London, aboard a paddle steamer on Lake Coniston and in Boston, USA.

In September 1998, we welcomed fellow theatre members from the Little Theatre Guild of Great Britain when we hosted a one-day workshop with a pantomime theme. Visitors from Questors Theatre, Ealing; Nomad Players, Horsley; and the Lindley Players, Whitstable joined guest speakers, Paul Harris and playwright Kevin Wood for the event.

Over the years, we have entertained a large number of Mayors and their escorts from Gillingham and Medway, as well as Paul Clark, Labour MP for Gillingham, and the President of the National Operatic and Dramatic Association.

The rich variety of visitors over the past 40 years have added to the excitement and folklore of our lively theatre. We always have great pleasure in showing our guests around the building and take great pride in all that we have achieved over the years. If you have never visited the world's first Oasthouse Theatre, we extend a warm welcome to you to come to one of our productions or drop in to see us if you are ever in the area on a Tuesday or Thursday rehearsal night. Anytime in the next 40 years will be fine.